Triumph Dolomite

An Enthusiast's Guide

Triumph Dolomite

An Enthusiast's Guide

Matthew Vale

THE CROWOOD PRESS

First published in 2015 by
The Crowood Press Ltd
Ramsbury, Marlborough
Wiltshire SN8 2HR

www.crowood.com

© Matthew Vale 2015

All rights reserved. No part of this publication may be reproduced or transmitted in any form or by any means, electronic or mechanical, including photocopy, recording, or any information storage and retrieval system, without permission in writing from the publishers.

British Library Cataloguing-in-Publication Data
A catalogue record for this book is available from the British Library.

ISBN 978 1 84797 893 6

Typeset and designed by D & N Publishing, Baydon, Wiltshire.

Printed and bound in Singapore by Craft Print International

CONTENTS

Acknowledgements and Picture Credits — 6

Timeline of the Triumph Company — 7

CHAPTER 1 DESIGN AND DEVELOPMENT OF THE DOLOMITE FAMILY — 9

CHAPTER 2 ANATOMY OF A SPORTS SALOON – TECHNICAL DESCRIPTION OF THE DOLOMITE FAMILY — 32

CHAPTER 3 THE DOLOMITE'S ANCESTORS – MODEL BY MODEL — 74

CHAPTER 4 THE DOLOMITES – MODEL BY MODEL — 95

CHAPTER 5 THE COMPETITION HISTORY — 119

CHAPTER 6 OWNING AND RUNNING — 129

Dolomite Clubs — 140

Bibliography — 141

Index — 142

ACKNOWLEDGEMENTS AND PICTURE CREDITS

The use of owners' experiences is an important part of all my books, so many thanks are due to Terry and Guy Stockley, James Shepard, Michael Soubry, Howard Rose, Clive and Gillian Raven, and Paul Wood for access to their cars and memories, and for allowing me to write about their experiences of running their Triumph saloons.

I would like to thank and acknowledge the British Motor Industry Heritage Trust for their help in producing this book, especially in the provision of original photographs of the Triumph prototypes, and access to the SD2 and Michelotti prototypes to help with my research. Further details of the Trust can be found at bmiht.co.uk. Thanks are also due to Andy Gilberg at the March archive site (marchives.com) for the pictures of the Unipart Formula 3 cars and information on the team. Finally I want to thank my wife Julia and daughter Elizabeth for putting up with me writing another book.

© BMIHT: All publicity material and photographs originally produced for/by the British Leyland Motor Corporation, British Leyland Ltd and Rover Group including all its subsidiary companies is the copyright of the British Motor Industry Heritage Trust and is reproduced in this publication with their permission. Permission to use images does not imply the assignment of copyright, and anyone wishing to re-use this material should contact BMIHT for permission to do so.

TIMELINE OF THE TRIUMPH COMPANY

1884	Siegfried Bettmann sets up his original company, S. Bettmann & Company, primarily importing sewing machines
1886	The company starts selling bicycles made for them by the William Andrews company; S. Bettmann & Company is renamed 'Triumph'
1887	Bettmann meets Mauritz Johan Schulte. Triumph expands into the Earls Court factory in Much Park Street, Coventry, and starts to manufacture its own bicycles. The company is renamed 'Triumph Cycle Company'
1902	Triumph produces its first motorcycle powered by a Belgium-built Minerva 2¼hp engine
1905	Triumph produces its own motorcycle engine, a 3hp unit
1907	Triumph goes public and moves to a larger factory complex on both sides of Priory Road, Coventry
1914–1918	Wartime production of motorcycles result in some 30,000 550cc belt-driven machines being supplied to the War Office. They are nicknamed the 'Trusty Triumphs' by the troops
1921–1928	Triumph manufactures the Ricardo-designed 4-valve head Triumph Ricardo 499cc single-cylinder motorcycle, a very advanced design for the time
1921	Dawson Motor Company acquired by Triumph, based at Clay Lane, Stoke in Coventry
1923	Triumph introduces its first car, the 10/20
1927	Triumph launches the 832cc Super Seven, an Austin Seven competitor
1933	Donald Healey joins Triumph as Experimental Manager
1934	Triumph first uses the 'Dolomite' name in the 1934 Gloria Dolomite Special
1934	A Triumph Gloria wins the Monte Carlo Rally Light Car Class and the Coupe des Alpes (Alpine Trial 1100cc class)
1934	Healey-designed Triumph Dolomite supercharged straight eight produced
1936	Motorcycle business sold to Jack Sangster
1936	New saloon range named 'Dolomite' introduced; Triumph records record losses of £212,104
1939	Triumph goes into receivership and is sold to Sheffield-based T.W. Ward and Company
1939	T.W. Ward turns the ex-Triumph factories over to war work
1940	Coventry Blitz flattens much of the ex-Triumph factories
1944	Standard buys the remains of Triumph and sells off the bomb-damaged premises in Coventry
1946	Brand-new Triumph Roadster and 1800 Saloon introduced and built in the Standard Triumph Canley site
1949	Triumph Mayflower introduced and Roadster discontinued
1953	TR2 sports car introduced

TIMELINE OF THE TRIUMPH COMPANY

1953	Standard Eight introduced, the first car to use the 'SC' engine later seen in the 1300 and 1500
1958	Standard Vignale introduced as a face-lift of the Vanguard Phase III; first Standard Triumph car styled by Michelotti
1959	Triumph Herald introduced, marking the beginning of the end of the use of the 'Standard' name on cars and the first complete new model styled by Michelotti
1960	Takeover of Standard by Leyland Motors
1963	Introduction of Triumph 2000 Saloon replacing the Standard Vanguard range and marking the end of the use of the 'Standard' name on cars
1965	Introduction of Triumph 1300 Saloon
1966	Leyland takeover of Rover
1966	British Motor Holdings (BMH) takeover of Jaguar
1968	Leyland and BMH merger resulting in the creation of British Leyland Motor Company (BLMC)
1970	Triumph 1500 front-wheel-drive Saloon and rear-wheel-drive Toledo launched
1972	Triumph Dolomite 1850 launched
1973	Triumph Dolomite Sprint launched
1975	Ryder Report into the state of British Leyland; results in state takeover of British Leyland
1976	Toledo 1500 and 1500 TC renamed 'Dolomite'
1977	Michael Edwards appointed head of British Leyland and instigates recovery plan
1978	British Leyland (BL) name adopted for the company
1978	BL approaches Honda for collaboration
1979	BL and Honda agree to collaboration; first project is the Triumph Acclaim
1980	Dolomite family of cars ceases production; Triumph plant at Canley closed
1981	Launch of the Triumph Acclaim, based on the Honda Ballade and built at the old Morris plant at Cowley – the last Triumph-badged car to be built

CHAPTER ONE

DESIGN AND DEVELOPMENT OF THE DOLOMITE FAMILY

INTRODUCTION

By the mid-1970s the Triumph name was firmly under the control of British Leyland, but still had a good reputation for producing both traditional sports cars and sporting saloons. One of its acknowledged strengths was in identifying niche markets and producing distinctive, sporty and well-engineered cars to fill them. The Triumph Dolomite of the 1970s was the ultimate medium-range Triumph saloon, which carried Triumph's reputation for quality, sporting saloon cars through the dark days of British Leyland. The Dolomite's final – and, in the opinion of many, the best – incarnation was as the Dolomite Sprint, a car with a groundbreaking overhead-cam sixteen-valve engine and a performance that was significantly better than that of many more expensive rivals. Apart from its advanced sixteen-valve engine the Dolomite Sprint was a thoroughly conventional but slightly dated-looking four-door saloon, with a front engine and rear-wheel drive via a live rear axle. However, its original ancestor, the Triumph 1300 of 1965, had been an innovative and advanced small saloon car with modern Italian styling, upmarket interior and equipment, front-wheel drive and sophisticated independent suspension front and rear.

The introduction of the Triumph 1300 in 1965 marked the birth of a dynasty of cars that would take Triumph into new market niches and demonstrate the technical ingenuity, quality and performance that were Triumph trademarks. In the 1960s Triumph was a thriving and successful business. Having been taken over by the Leyland Motor Company in 1961, Triumph had the financial clout behind it to introduce the all-new upmarket six-cylinder 2000 saloon in 1963 to complement its smaller Herald saloon, and its Spitfire and TR4 sports cars.

At this time Triumph's TR range of two-seat sports cars had established Triumph's sporting reputation; the Spitfire was the bestseller in the small, cheap sports-car market. The Herald range had re-established the name in the small saloon market; and the newly introduced 2000 was quick to establish the Triumph name in the upmarket sporty executive saloon sector. This left a gap in the market between the small, two-door Herald and the much larger executive four-door 2000 saloon. In 1965, Triumph's medium or mid-sized saloon range was launched with the introduction of the four-door, front-wheel-drive 1300, which, in terms of price and size, slotted neatly in between the Herald and the 2000. Powered by a 1296cc 61bhp four-cylinder engine, and equipped with up-to-date independent front and rear suspension, the car was styled by Italian Giovanni Michelotti, with a look that was based on that of the current Triumph 2000 large saloon. The car was an immediate success, and the range was expanded in 1967 with the 1300 TC, which was a twin-carburettor version of the 1300 giving 75bhp, a useful performance increase over the original 1300.

The first major change to the range came in 1970, when the two 1300s were replaced with a pair of face-lifted models, the 1500 and the Toledo. The 1500 had a new, lengthened four-door body shell with a much larger boot, while the Toledo was a two-door that retained the 1300's short boot; it gained four doors in 1972.

The front-wheel-drive Triumph 1300 was the first of the Triumph medium-sized saloon cars. Styled by Italian maestro Michelotti, the car changed little during its production.

The ultimate Dolomite, with the sixteen-valve Sprint engine. The rear-wheel-drive Dolomite was the final incarnation of the Triumph medium-sized saloon.

Herald Coupé. At the time, the two-door Herald was Triumph's smallest saloon.

The Triumph 2000 was the 1300's big brother – it was larger and had a six-cylinder engine.

The 1300 was a neat design, with good accommodation that was easily accessed. The short boot of the early design is obvious in this shot.

The 1300 was replaced by the rear-wheel-drive Toledo, which was initially a two-door. While the front-end styling was revised, it retained the short tail of the 1300.

The 1500 had, as the name suggests, a larger 1500cc engine and retained the 1300's front-wheel drive, but it had a dead rear axle rather than the 1300's independent set-up. The Toledo was rear-wheel drive. This pair of cars then led to the Dolomite 1850 – introduced in 1972 – which used Triumph's new 1854cc slant four overhead-cam motor, a four-speed gearbox with optional

The Toledo was also offered in four-door form. The side profile reveals its strong resemblance to the 1300.

The rear-wheel-drive Dolomite was introduced in 1972. It was a compact sporting saloon with Triumph's new 1850cc overhead cam engine.

THE COMPETITION

When the 1300 was introduced, in 1965, it was designed to compete with the top-of-the-range small saloons in various ranges. The comparisons are interesting. At June 1968 prices, the 1300 cost £868 on the road, and the 1300 TC was £909. The top-of-the-range Austin Morris 1300 was the Vanden Plas 1300, costing £1,065; the Ford Escort 1300 GT was £826 and the Vauxhall Viva 90SL was £793. The dated Hillman Minx was £829 and the Austin 1300 four-door was a competitive £775. Foreign competition was not so common in the sub-£1,000 price bracket, but there was an Opel Kadett four-door for £877 and the Saab 96 de-luxe for £935, while the Volvo 131 saloon was a massive £1,133.

In 1977, with the range now called Dolomite, British Leyland issued a neat little *Product Guide* to its sales force. The Dolomite section identified the various cars that competed with each of the Dolomites and gave a raft of details to help the salesperson persuade the prospective customer to go for the Triumph.

The main rivals to the Dolomite 1300 were named as the Ford Escort 1300 GL four-door, the Vauxhall Viva 1300 GLS, the Citroen GS Club and the Renault 12 TL. The text noted that the 1300's touring fuel consumption was compatible with that of its rivals, but was much better when the car was driven hard. The Dolomite's 12-month warranty period was twice as long as that of the French cars, the 1300's fuel capacity was larger, and it was safer with its laminated windscreen and head restraints.

The Dolomite 1500 was compared to the Ford Cortina 1600 GL, the Vauxhall Cavalier 1600 L, the Peugeot 304 and the Fiat 131 1600 Special. Again, the warranty was identified as being longer than that of the French cars. In addition, the performance and the turning circle of the Dolomite were superior to those of most of the opposition.

The 1500HL was compared with the Escort 1600 Ghia, the Chrysler Alpine S, the Volkswagen Passat 1300 L and the Alfasud Ti. The equipment levels of the Dolomite took centre stage in the comparison, along with the warranty, safety features and lower insurance group.

With the Dolomite 1850 HL the competitors moved upmarket – the Ford Cortina 2000 Ghia, the Fiat 132 GLS 1800, the Audi 80 GLS and the Lancia Beta 1600. Performance, with a class-winning 0–60mph time for the Dolomite, was the first advantage identified, along with a lower insurance group, better towing fuel consumption and longer range.

Finally, the *Product Guide* pitched the Sprint against an interesting selection of 1970s performance cars: the Ford Capri 2000 Ghia and Escort RS1800 Custom, the BMW 320 and the Lancia Beta Coupé 1600. Even with two coupés in the mix, the 0–60 time and top speed of the Sprint were better than all the competitors', although the in-gear acceleration of the Sprint was beaten by the Escort, BMW and Lancia. The main comparison related to the equipment levels of the Sprint, which were far superior to those of the others.

Clearly, the Triumph medium-sized saloons were a competitive and exciting range of cars that could justifiably compete with the best the market could offer.

The Vanden Plas 1300 was a luxury-specification BMC 1300 with a prominent and posh grille. It was a competitor to the upmarket Triumph 1300.

DESIGN AND DEVELOPMENT OF THE DOLOMITE FAMILY ■ 15

competitors

	Ford Capri 2000 Ghia	Ford Escort RS 1800 Custom	BMW 320	Lancia Beta Coupé 1600
	1993 cc BHP 98 Torque 111 OHC	1834 cc BHP 115 Torque 126 Twin OHC 4 valve	1990 cc BHP 109 Torque 117 OHC	1585 cc BHP 100 Torque 98 Twin OHC
	Front—Ind McPherson Strut Rear—Leaf	Front—Ind McPherson Strut Rear—Leaf	Front—Ind Coil Rear—Ind Coil	Front—Ind Coil Rear—Ind Coil
	Disc/Drum/Servo	Disc/Drum/Servo	Disc/Drum/Servo	Disc/Disc/Servo
	4 speed synchro floor mounted	4 speed synchro floor mounted	4 speed synchro floor mounted	5 speed synchro floor mounted
	Length—14 ft 1 in Width—5 ft 6·9 in	Length—13 ft 0·6 in Width—5 ft 2·8 in	Length—14 ft 3 in Width—5 ft 3 in	Length—13 ft 1 in Width—5 ft 5 in

British Leyland gave their salesmen details of the rivals to all their models. The Capri 2000, Escort RS1800, BMW 320 and Lancia Beta Coupé were all seen as competing with the Dolomite Sprint.

Dolomite Sprint

Engine	1998 cc BHP 127 Torque 122 SOHC 4 v
Suspension	Front—Ind Coil Rear—Coil
Brakes	Disc/Drum/Servo
Gearbox	4 speed syn floor mtd overdrive on 3rd & top
Dimensions	Length—13 ft 6 in Width—5 ft 2·5 in

The overall performance of the Sprint is significantly better than three of the four competitors used in the comparison and only the specially tuned Escort RS 1800 has comparable figures.

— The top speed of the Sprint at 112·7 mph is over 6 mph faster than the Capri Ghia and BMW 320, and over 5 mph faster than the Lancia Beta Coupé.

— The Sprint's 0–60 mph time of 8·4 seconds is faster than all of its competitors, 2·1 seconds quicker than the BMW and 2·0 seconds quicker than the Capri.

The Sprint has twice the warranty period of the Lancia Beta and none of the competitors can match the benefits of Supercover and AA membership.

Alloy wheels, tinted glass, vinyl roof and push button radio are standard on the Sprint but are not included in the basic specification of the Escort RS 1800, BMW 320 or the Lancia Beta.

The basic specification of the Sprint includes opening front quarter lights, height adjustable driver's seat, rear seat centre arm-rest and wood veneer door cappings, features which cannot be found on any of the competitors.

The salesman's guide also gave a summary of the advantages of the BL cars, including the Sprint.

overdrive, a live rear axle placed in the 1500-style long-boot body and a luxurious but sporty well-equipped interior.

The range was expanded and rationalized to be all rear-wheel drive in 1973 with the front-wheel-drive 1500 being dropped, and the introduction of the Dolomite Sprint and the 1500 TC. The Sprint used the sixteen-valve version of the Dolomite slant four engine, which gave a significant performance boost to the range. The 1500 TC was

16 ■ DESIGN AND DEVELOPMENT OF THE DOLOMITE FAMILY

A 1500 HL with aftermarket alloy wheels. As the 1970s progressed, Triumph named all its medium saloons Dolomites.

equipped with a more powerful twin-carburettor version of the 1500 saloon's engine, which was used to drive the rear wheels via a conventional gearbox and live rear axle. The choice of models was rationalized in 1976, with the entire range being renamed Dolomite. These cars remained in production until 1980.

The replacement for the range was a re-badged Honda, the Triumph Acclaim, which was produced between 1981 and 1984 and was, at the time of writing, the last car to bear the Triumph name.

BACKGROUND

Triumph as a manufacturer was expert at seeking out niche markets and filling them with well-designed models, and this trend was particularly visible throughout the 1960s. Having made its image for producing successful sports cars in the 1950s with the TR range, Triumph, under the auspices of its Standard owner, produced the small but comfortable Herald saloon range in 1959. This replaced the small Standard saloons and marked the start of the exclusive use of the Triumph name for Standard products. The Herald was soon joined by the Spitfire sports car and the refined six-cylinder-engined Herald-based Vitesse sports saloon. The early 1960s saw the introduction of the large upmarket 2000 saloon, which replaced the aged large Standard saloon car offerings. This model cemented Triumph's position as a purveyor of quality cars aimed firmly at the gap between the bread-and-butter mass-market Austins/Morrises, Fords and Vauxhalls and the upper-crust Jaguars, while also offering prices that undercut the competition from Italian and German manufacturers.

Triumph's biggest rival for market position was in fact Rover. While the Rover 2000 was also firmly aimed at the middle luxury market and competed

The Rover 2000.

directly with the Triumph 2000 range, Triumph differentiated its product from Rover's by emphasizing its sporting pedigree. This, along with the touch of luxury, was intended to appeal to an executive customer who was probably a bit younger than Rover's 'Bank Manager' type.

Triumph as a company had been in existence since 1885. After manufacturing sewing machines, bicycles and motorbikes, it started to produce cars in the 1920s. By the mid-1930s, it was producing a bewildering range of cars but was not making any money. By June 1939, it had gone into receivership, despite selling off, in 1936 to Jack Sangster, its motorcycle business, including its Priory Street factory in Coventry. The remaining car manufacturing company was bought up by Yorkshire engineering conglomerate T. W. Ward on 1 September 1939, just two days before Britain's entry into the Second World War. The takeover and the need for war production meant that Triumph's largest production plant, the Gloria works at Holbrooks Lane, Coventry, was quickly sold to the H.M. Hobson company and the British government. It was soon turned over to the production of aircraft carburettors. This left only the much smaller Stoke works, which was at the time producing aircraft components for Armstrong Whitworth, in the hands of Triumph.

When the Germans bombed the centre of Coventry, in November 1940, the Stoke works were severely damaged, most of the car tooling was destroyed and all production ceased. In 1944, Standard stepped in and bought the remains of Triumph, which by then comprised little more than the bombed-out factory, the name and trademarks and remaining goodwill. Almost immediately, the old factory site was sold on, with just the Triumph name being retained. Standard's boss, Sir John Black, had plans to use the name to compete with Sir William Lyons's Jaguar concern. Before the war Standard had supplied chassis and engines to Lyons for his 'SS' cars, but Lyons had bought the tooling for Standard's old six-cylinder engines in 1942 as a quick route to bringing all his manufacturing in house. By the end of the war, Lyons obviously could not continue in business with those 'SS' initials – the negative connotations and their association with Hitler's Nazis were just too much – so in 1945 he adopted the name 'Jaguar'.

Sir John Black had approached Lyons with a view to a merger during the war but had been firmly rejected. The purchase of the Triumph name gave him the means to compete with SS/Jaguar with a premium performance brand that would complement Standard's post-war range of worthy saloons – which could never really be described as sporting! However, Triumph's first post-war models did not really conform to the right profile. The 1800/2000 range comprised a large 'sit-up-and-beg' saloon (later named the Renown) and the Roadster.

The Saloon had so-called 'razor-edge' styling, carried over from pre-war days, with a prominent bonnet, separate flowing front wings and running boards, and hard straight creases to delineate the body lines. This gave it a stately but somewhat dated appearance. The Roadster had more rounded styling, although it kept the pre-war-style front wings and running boards. It was an open-top tourer, which could accommodate five passengers at a pinch – three people on the front bench seat and two passengers squeezed into a dicky seat on the rear deck. This Roadster was made famous when it featured in the 1980s BBC TV series *Bergerac*, driven by the Jersey-based detective played by actor John Nettles. It had much more curvy styling than the razor-edged saloon and, while its relatively small four-cylinder engine did not give it a particularly good performance, it was a characterful and attractive car.

The styling of Triumph's first post-war cars was firmly rooted in the pre-war era. The Triumph Renown was a typical example.

The Triumph Roadster was more of a grand touring car than a sports car.

If Triumph's Renown Saloon and the Roadster were not too sporting, Triumph's third post-war model was even less so. The Mayflower, a small two-door saloon, again with 'razor-edge' styling and luxury wood and leather interior, could best be described as a mini Bentley or Rolls Royce. Powered by a 1247cc four-cylinder side-valve engine producing a mere 38bhp, which was unique to the model, the Mayflower was not a performance machine. Introduced in 1949, the car was intended to fulfil perceived market demand for a small economical upmarket saloon to be sold alongside the planned sports TR2. Unfortunately, although it was quite popular in the UK, where it retains a dedicated following in the classic car scene, the car flopped in its intended market, the USA. It was phased out of production in 1953, just as Triumph's first two-seater sports car, the TR2, was introduced. The TR models were aimed squarely at the US market for small, two-seat sports cars. In the early post-war years, that market had been gobbling up as many MG 'T' series cars as it could get. The TR2 was a neat two-seater with a four-cylinder 2-litre engine (based on the Ferguson tractor unit that was supplied by Standard). It had 'full-width' styling, making it bang up to date in comparison with the distinctly pre-war 'square-rigger' styling of the MG TC, TD and TF, with their narrow bodies, separate front wings and running boards.

The Roadster was produced only up to 1950 and by 1954 the Mayflower and Renown ranges had also been dropped, leaving the TR as the only Triumph car in the Standard range. This gave the Triumph brand an exclusively sporting image, which was carried through the 1950s with the evolution of the TR range, via the TR3 through to the modern-looking TR4, with its bluff-faced style and wind-up windows and, in later versions, independent rear suspension. The sporting image was enhanced by

The first post-war Triumph sports car was the TR2. This TR3 shows the sporty lines and neat styling.

the company running TR2-based cars at Le Mans in 1955, with all three cars finishing, and by many rally wins. TRs continued to compete at Le Mans and, while the new TRS cars finished in the 1960 event but did not quite make the required distance, all three finished in the rankings in the 1961 event. This success heralded the debut of the TR4.

The TR range continued to be the only Triumph-badged cars produced by Standard until 1959 when the Triumph Herald was introduced. This was a small four-seat saloon car (that could fit five at a squeeze), introduced as a replacement for the Standard Eight and Ten ranges and initially produced as a two-door saloon or coupé. Powered by a 35bhp 948cc four-cylinder engine, developed from the Standard 10 unit (the SC engine originally produced in 1952), and styled by Italian maestro Giovanni Michelotti, the Herald featured a separate chassis and bolt-together body.

The Herald's chassis and separate body construction was chosen by Triumph as an expedient as they could not rely on any single body manufacturer to supply them with a monocoque shell. Triumph's traditional supplier, Fisher and Ludlow, had been taken over by BMC, who refused to supply a competitor. Its other major supplier, Pressed Steel, did not have the capacity. As a result, Triumph had to source the various body panels from a number of suppliers, including Pressed Steel and Mulliners, and build up the bodies in-house. However, this method of construction was inefficient and led to quality issues around panel fit and sealing.

Increasing the bore of the original 948cc engine in 1961, from 63mm to 69mm, increased engine capacity to 1147cc and power output to 39bhp and gave a performance boost. Along with the introduction of estate and convertible body styles to complement the saloon and coupés, Standard now had a versatile small saloon that could meet most market demands. In 1963 a raised compression ratio increased engine power to 51bhp, and in 1965 a further increase in the engine's bore, to

The Herald and 6-cylinder Vitesse range were Triumph's small saloons. The Vitesse was a refined and fast offering and was the first of Triumph's sporting saloon family.

73.7mm, gave a capacity of 1296cc and 61bhp to improve performance further. This was the next stage in the birth of the true ancestor of Triumph's Dolomite range, the Triumph 1300 Saloon.

THE ANCESTOR OF THE DOLOMITE

After the Herald had been introduced, in 1959, Standard, having had a period of prosperity in the 1950s, suddenly hit the stops financially. They had spent a large amount of cash on acquisitions to consolidate their supplier base, had just started producing the Herald and were committed to spending a significant amount of money to get the 2000 Saloon project into production when sales fell off. The Vanguard saloon was old and almost unsellable, and the Herald was failing to meet its sales projections and was developing a reputation for poor quality. Despite announcing profits of over £1.8 million for 1959–1960, the company was in dire straits. Leyland Motors came to the rescue in the autumn of 1961 with an offer to buy the Standard company; the sale was completed by November 1961, stabilizing the company and enabling it to get back on course. The first result of the takeover was the introduction of the Triumph 2000 Saloon in 1963, which was only possible with the backing of cash from Leyland. Management at the time also recognized the need for a Herald replacement due to the poor sales and work commenced on what would become the Triumph 1300 in 1961. At the time Triumph used four-letter code words to identify their projects, and this project was given the name 'Ajax'.

After the Leyland takeover, Herald quality improved and sales started to pick up. As the design team was busy with the Spitfire, TR4A and 2000, the need for a Herald replacement evaporated and development of the 1300 was very much on the back burner. A smaller version of the 1300 with a truncated tail, code-named 'Manx', was considered in the mid-1960s, but was not put into production.

While the 1300 was originally supposed to be a successor to the Herald, once the new 2000 was launched it became clear that there was a market for a high-quality, technically advanced medium-sized saloon car that would fit neatly between the 2000 and the Herald.

As part of Standard's acquisition programme in the late 1950s, the company had bought Hall Engineering, which made Herald body pressings and was based in Speke near Liverpool. The new factory was named 'Liverpool Number 1' and was soon developed into a body-pressing and -building plant. Triumph now had its own in-house capability and capacity to produce a new one-piece body shell, avoiding the quality and fit issues of the Herald's separate chassis and bolted-up body.

The 1300 design concept evolved to be a medium-sized, four-door saloon that would slot into the gap in the Triumph range, and would retain a family resemblance to the 2000. It was styled by Michelotti, following a brief to produce a 'junior Triumph 2000'. From an engineering and design perspective, the car would have to have a monocoque body shell, have four doors and would have front-wheel drive. The choice of monocoque construction was made for two very valid reasons. First, there was a certain amount of customer resistance to the Herald's construction with its separate chassis and bolt-up body, which was felt to be (and indeed was) old-fashioned, and had led to quality issues relating to panel fit and water leaks. Second, a monocoque was cheaper, lighter and easier to construct. In its role as a larger, more technically advanced car than the Herald, the 1300 was specified with front-wheel drive, both to match the Austin/Morris 1100/1300 range, which was announced in 1962, and to provide the maximum amount of interior space.

One of the original Michelotti design proposals for the 1300.

A later design, showing a close resemblance to the final production model.

Another view of the later design proposal, again close to the final model but with only two doors.

MICHELOTTI'S DESIGN

As had been Triumph's policy in the early 1960s, the Italian designer Giovanni Michelotti was commissioned to design Triumph's new mid-range saloon, following his exemplary job on the then new Triumph 2000. Triumph's design team under Harry Webster laid out the mechanical side of the design, defined the position of the scuttle and seats and presented these to Michelotti with a brief to produce a junior 2000. They also tied Michelotti down to a short bonnet and boot. Webster recalled in an interview in *Autocar* magazine (18 February 1966) how this had been the hardest part of managing Michelotti – constraining the length of the car to avoid him putting lots of 'beautiful things' on the front! There were a number of iterations of the design until an acceptable one was approved by Triumph. The initial design brief had asked for both a two-door and a four-door body. Eventually, as the design brief evolved and the two-door option fell by the wayside as the Herald sales picked up, the four-door saloon layout, larger than the Herald but smaller than the 2000, was settled on. At that point Michelotti produced a full-sized wooden model of the car and the production drawings were taken from this. Webster was also fulsome in his praise of Michelotti's practical side; he recalled how Michelotti understood the need to reproduce his design using press tools, and recounted how there were virtually no changes to the design as the bodywork was 'productionized'.

FROM THE 1300 TO THE SPRINT

The 1300 established the Triumph name in the medium-sized saloon segment and was positioned as an upmarket offering with good equipment levels – a quality image with a sporting edge. The model fitted neatly between the Herald and the 2000 saloon, had a strong family resemblance to the 2000 and was a success from the start of production in 1965. The sporting side was enhanced by the introduction of the 1300 TC with twin carburettors, and a significant performance boost and a brake servo as standard in 1967. With its front-wheel drive and relatively sophisticated independent rear suspension, excellent equipment levels and quality image, the 1300 range gave Triumph a firm place in the upmarket section of the mid-range saloon market, competing with the likes of the Austin/Morris 1100 and 1300, the Ford Escort and Vauxhall Viva. The 1300 was offered only in four-door form.

In 1970 the 1300 range was replaced with a new pair of face-lifted models, the Toledo (Project Manx II) and the 1500 (Project Ajax III). Both cars gained a restyled front end – what was to become the Dolomite front end – with a flat panel ahead of the forward-opening bonnet and a pair of air inlets divided by a central divider, which carried a badge giving the model name. This design was carried forward on the whole Dolomite family. The Toledo was essentially a down-specified 1300, with rear-wheel drive, and a new two-door body shell that retained the 'short' boot and rear styling of the 1300 – the new nose meant that the Toledo was a couple of inches longer than the 1300. It was also fitted with a pair of oblong headlamps. The model was essentially a Herald replacement and was priced slightly above the 13/60 Herald saloon, which was soon to be discontinued (£876 for the Toledo as opposed to £816 for the 12/60 Herald, according to *Autocar* magazine). It was able to utilize the 1296cc engine and four-speed gearbox as used in the Herald and Spitfire, which was cheaper than the FWD set-up of the 1300. At the rear, the 1300's complex independent rear suspension was replaced with a simple live axle, suspended using coil springs and located with two trailing and two semi-trailing arms. The Toledo gained an extra pair of doors in October 1972, by which time it was Triumph's base model.

The 1500 Saloon retained the 1300's front-wheel drive, and had an enlarged version of the 1300's engine displacing 1493cc and 61bhp. Its

DESIGN AND DEVELOPMENT OF THE DOLOMITE FAMILY 25

This 1967 sketch shows Michelotti's redesign of the 1300, which resulted in the 1500/Dolomite family.

The rear view of the 1967 restyle shows there is some more work needed before arriving at the ultimate shape.

The Triumph 1500 was the first of the Dolomite family to have the long-boot body, and was the last to have front-wheel drive.

lengthened body shell added an extra 7 inches to its length, all but an inch or so behind the rear wheels, giving a larger boot. The 1500 also lost the 1300's independent rear suspension, which was replaced with a cheaper dead-beam-type axle, and had four 5¾-inch (14.5-cm) diameter round headlamps in pairs at the outside end of each front grille. Probably the most significant change to the range came in 1972, with the introduction of the Dolomite. This resurrected a famous name from Triumph's past – the first Dolomite, produced in 1934 and designed to compete in the 1935 Monte Carlo Rally, was an exotic, supercharged eight-cylinder road racer, based closely on the 1931 Alfa Romeo 8C 2300. Only three of the Straight 8 Dolomites were built, but in 1937 Triumph produced a range of sports saloons named Dolomite, which were powered by more conventional six- and four-cylinder engines. Following this, the Dolomite name became associated with Triumph's sporting saloons rather than with its road racer. One distinctive feature of these Dolomites was the extravagant, chromed 'Waterfall' grille, which marked the model out from the opposition.

The 1972 Dolomite was a similar kind of car. It was powered by a completely new engine – the Triumph 1850cc slant four single overhead-camshaft unit, which had an output of 91bhp and endowed the saloon with an excellent performance, with a top speed of about 100mph (160km/h). The body shell was based on the long-boot version used on the 1500 saloon, but the big difference on the 1500 was the fact that the Dolomite had rear-wheel drive, with a live axle, coil springs and four link attachment as in the Toledo.

The Dolomite name was used on Triumph's pre-war sports saloons. This example shows the stylish 'Waterfall' grille.

With a black 'egg-box' grille, twin headlamps, black vinyl trim on the rear 'C' pillars and a black rear panel, the Dolomite was distinctive. The styling of the interior, with a full set of instruments in a walnut-veneer dash as well as cloth sports seats, added weight to the car's sporting pedigree. The four-door body shell with large boot made the car a practical but sporting and upmarket alternative to the Morris Marina, Ford Cortina and Hillman Hunter, and an attractive option to those customers considering a BMW, Alfa Romeo or Lancia sporting saloon of the time.

The 1850 Dolomite was well received by the public and the press, and its success led to the introduction of the Dolomite Sprint in 1973. This was an even faster car than the Dolomite with a sixteen-valve development of the slant four engine, which was also enlarged to a full 2 litres, giving an impressive 127bhp. It kept the standard Dolomite's rear-wheel drive and had a beefed-up drive train and alloy wheels fitted as standard.

In the same year the 1500 TC was introduced. While using a twin-carb version of the 1500's engine, giving 64bhp, this model was rear-wheel drive and went upmarket with the Dolomite interior and exterior trim, including the Dolomite's dashboard with full instrumentation, egg-box grille and twin headlamps. In 1976, the range was rationalized and the Dolomite name and badging were adopted; the front-wheel-drive 1500 was dropped, leaving all the cars in the range with rear-wheel drive and the longer Dolomite body shell. The Toledo became the Dolomite 1300, with four doors, the Toledo-style front end with a pair of oblong headlamps, and a low-specification interior

The new front end on the Dolomite gave the car an aggressive and sporty appearance.

The Dolomite Sprint was understated, but was the first British mass-production car to have alloy wheels as standard and a 16-valve engine.

The entry-level model of the final Dolomite range was the Dolomite 1300. Its single headlights are a recognition point.

PRODUCTION FIGURES FOR THE DOLOMITE FAMILY OF CARS

Model	Number	Years
1300	113,008	1965–1970
1300 TC	35,342	1968–1970
1300 (export only 1500cc)	3,676	1968–1970
Toledo	113,294	1970–1976
Toledo 1500	5,888	1971–1976
1500	66,353	1970–1973
1500 TC	25,549	1973–1976
Dolomite/ Dolomite 1850	79,010	1972–1980
Dolomite Sprint	22,941	1973–1980
Dolomite 1300	32,031	1976–1980
Dolomite 1500/1500 HL	70,021	1976–1980

with no rev counter. The rear-wheel-drive 1500 TC could be had in two trim ranges: as the standard 'Dolomite 1500', which, apart from the twin-carb 1493cc engine, was effectively the same specification as the 1300 Dolomite; and as the '1500 HL Dolomite', which was virtually identical in specification (apart from the engine) and appearance to the original Dolomite. The original Dolomite 1850 was renamed 'Dolomite 1850 HL' from early 1976, while the Sprint remained largely unchanged, being kept on as the top-of-the-range model.

The final range of five rear-wheel-drive Dolomites (1300, 1500, 1500 HL, 1850 HL and Sprint) remained broadly unchanged until production ended in 1980.

THE END OF THE LINE

When the 1300 came to the market, in 1965, it was the first of a range of medium-sized saloons that would give Triumph and British Leyland a strong presence in the sporting saloon market right up to 1980. The line begun by the 1300 expanded over the years, and led to the introduction of the sporting Dolomite range. The Dolomite was the last of the 'real' Triumph saloons, as the 2000 range was discontinued in 1977. With the constraints placed on British Leyland, due to its atrocious financial position, the number of manufacturing plants and model lines had to be reduced, and Triumph bore the brunt of these cuts. The Dolomite range was long in the tooth and needed replacement, but British Leyland's finances meant there was nothing in the pipeline. Falling sales meant that production of the Dolomite ended in 1980.

The Triumph name was continued for a few more years with the Acclaim, a re-badged Honda Ballade. This car was assembled at the old Morris plant at Cowley between 1981 and 1984, using a locally produced body shell and trim items, with virtually every other part of the car coming from Honda. The Acclaim was introduced only as a stop gap; the mass-market Austin Maestro hatchback would not be ready for production until 1983, so something was needed to fill that gap in the medium-range market. The Acclaim gave British Leyland an up-to-date car in the medium-saloon sector, and was actually quite successful. However, it was to be the last car to carry the Triumph badge, as the strategy at British Leyland (or Austin Rover, as it had become by 1981) was to use only Austin and Rover names for its mass-market cars. As a result, while the successor to the Triumph Acclaim was based on the next-generation Honda Ballade, it was badged as a Rover. The Honda-engined Rover 213 was produced from 1984 through to 1990. Along with the 216, powered by the home-produced 'S' series engine, it would help Austin Rover survive through the 1980s and continued the Rover/Honda collaboration that would sustain Austin Rover through the 1980s and 1990s.

The Honda-based Triumph Acclaim was the Dolomite family replacement. Introduced in 1981, it carried forward the Triumph tradition of small comfortable saloons but with 1300cc its performance was not scintillating.

DESIGN AND DEVELOPMENT OF THE DOLOMITE FAMILY   31

The Acclaim was replaced by the Rover 213/216 range in 1984. The 216 Vitesse resurrected the famous Triumph model name and its 1600 fuel-injected motor gave it a respectable performance.

CHAPTER TWO

ANATOMY OF A SPORTS SALOON – TECHNICAL DESCRIPTION OF THE DOLOMITE FAMILY

INTRODUCTION

This chapter looks at each element that made up the Dolomite family – body shell, engine, transmission and final drive, suspension and brakes – and gives an in-depth technical description, along with the changes that occurred throughout the models' long life. The Dolomite family was interesting from a technological viewpoint. The first and last of the family both boasted innovative and technically advanced features – the 1300 had a uniquely configured front-wheel drive and sophisticated independent rear suspension, while the Dolomite Sprint had a sixteen-valve engine with ingenious operation of the valves from a single camshaft. In between, however, the family was thoroughly conventional, with the majority of models reverting to rear-wheel drive with a live axle; even the front-wheel-drive 1500 lost the 1300's independent rear suspension and was given a dead-beam rear axle. However, even though the design philosophy was apparently timid, the result was an outstandingly successful family of cars that filled an important market niche for Leyland and British Leyland for over a decade.

THE DOLOMITE FAMILY BODY SHELL

The body shell was the defining common element of the Dolomite family of cars, but it underwent a number of changes throughout its lifetime. It started off with technically advanced front-wheel drive and fully independent rear suspension, and eventually had to accommodate a conventional front engine and rear-wheel-drive configuration with a live axle. There were four distinct variations of the shell, the first being the 1300's four-door unit with a short boot and front-wheel drive. The second, first seen on the 1500, was a four-door, long-boot version with front-wheel drive, and the third was the Toledo type with two doors (and later four doors), short boot and rear-wheel drive. The fourth variant was the final Dolomite type, with four doors, the long boot and rear-wheel drive. All of the various versions of the body shell were firmly based on the original 1300 shell, and the lineage is obvious if the first (1300) and last (Dolomite) of the line are compared.

The Triumph 1300 was Triumph's second monocoque-bodied saloon, following on from the successful Triumph 2000. The 1300's body shell was a relatively conventional monocoque design, styled by Giovanni Michelotti and made from pressed-steel panels welded together. With its four doors, front engine compartment and a rear luggage boot, it followed the format set by the 2000. It was in fact a thoroughly conventional-looking three-box design, in contrast to the BMC 1100/1300 range, which incorporated a more radical two-box design with the rear window and boot lid relatively neatly integrated to give good interior and boot space.

The 1300's monocoque was designed to be smaller than the 2000, in order to address the market sector below the larger saloon, but also at the same time to give good accommodation for passengers, offer reasonable boot space and accommodate a front-wheel-drive engine and gearbox. In fact, the

RIGHT: **The BMIHT Museum at Gaydon, Warwickshire, UK, has an immaculate 1300 in its collection.**

BELOW: **The Dolomite family floor pan had reinforcing cross sections and extensive pressings in the floor panels to make a light and rigid monocoque.**

1300's design had a passenger compartment that was only 1¼in (just over 3cm) shorter than the 2000's when measured from the toe board to the rear seat squab – and this was in a car that was some 18in (45cm) shorter overall. This was made possible by the compact design of the engine transmission unit, and by the shape and size of the boot, which was deep but short.

The body shell's main strength was provided by the two sills, which were made up of a sill reinforce plate sandwiched between a pair of inner and outer sill elements, forming a braced box-section member. The sill extended from the toe board backwards to the rear wheel arch. At the front a pair of chassis legs projected forwards to carry the engine sub-frame. The overall body structure was

The Dolomite's sills are important structural members. This shows the underside box section, with rust starting to penetrate the inner sill.

built up around the sills and front chassis members. These longitudinal members were braced by transverse cross members formed by the radiator grille surround, front scuttle, the front seat dais, rear seat pan and the boot-lid jamb, all of which featured various degrees of double skinning to give additional strength. The rest of the body strength was provided by the box-section 'A', 'B' and 'C' pillars, which transmitted stresses and loads into the roof panel. The four doors were conventional, with the fronts having separate opening quarter lights and fixed quarter lights in the rear. All four main windows were manually operated. The front and rear screens were produced in Triplex safety glass, as were the side windows.

The bonnet was front-hinged and opened forwards, and formed the top half of a front panel, the lower half of which sloped backwards and surmounted a narrow grille. At each side of the front there was a 7in (17.5cm) diameter headlamp, and under each headlamp a wraparound combined side light and indicator.

At the rear the boot lid opened on two hinges and the lid's lip extended down to the level of the boot floor, making loading easier. Under the boot floor lived the spare wheel, tools and the fuel tank.

The ventilation system relied on a series of vents above and outside the rear window in the roof overhang. When the car was moving, these vents were in a low-pressure area, and stale air was drawn out of the interior through a channel behind the rear parcel shelf, which was connected to the roof-mounted vents by channels inside the 'C' pillars.

The use of the front-wheel-drive engine and gearbox unit meant that the bonnet line had to be

The 1300 engine bay shows the engine, which is mounted relatively high, the front suspension turrets and the forward-hinged bonnet.

raised by some 1¾ inches (4.35cm) from what was considered to be ideal from a styling point of view, in order to accommodate the taller engine and transmission package. The main body shell incorporated pick-up points for the suspension with towers in the front inner wings to mount the top of the front suspension struts, and strengthened areas to receive the rubber-mounted front and rear sub-frames. The engine and transmission unit did not intrude into the passenger cabin; the gear lever emerged from under the dashboard and there was no transmission tunnel, resulting in a mainly flat floor pan in the passenger cabin.

A great deal of care was put into the design of the body shell to ensure that the car was quiet. According to Harry Webster, in an interview with journalist Roland Barker in *Autocar* magazine (18 February 1966 edition), panels in the body shell that would give noise problems were identified and modified to make them stiffer and change their resonant frequency, for example, by modifying with a styling feature. Webster also recalled how the design aimed for a very high torsional and bending stiffness – and it was certainly successful in this, since the complete body stiffness approached 6,000lb/ft per degree of twist but weighed only 510lb (231kg). In comparison, the contemporary Lotus Elan chassis, considered to be one of the best at the time, had a torsional stiffness of 4,300lb/ft per degree of movement. The 1300's engine, clutch, transmission, front suspension and steering were carried on a separate sub-frame, which was bolted to the main body shell using four conical rubber bushes. These were carefully tuned to damp out noise and vibration, again adding to the refinement of the final car.

The independent rear suspension, with its trailing arms and coil over dampers, was also mounted on to a sub-frame, in this case a wide 'V'-shaped affair, which was then rubber-mounted at three points to the body shell – one central mount utilizing a conical rubber mount and an outer mount

ABOVE: **The Dolomite's boot housed the fuel tank on the left and the spare wheel on the right, covered by a rigid panel. Here, the boot floor has rusted under the fuel tank due to water ingress.**

RIGHT: **A Dolomite styling feature was the black vinyl on the 'C' pillar, and a small round badge with either a 'D' or, in this case for the Sprint, the word 'SPRINT' on it. Note also the three rear air extractor vents on the rear lip of the roof and the Sprint's vinyl roof.**

36 ■ ANATOMY OF A SPORTS SALOON – TECHNICAL DESCRIPTION OF THE DOLOMITE FAMILY

The front-wheel-drive 1300's gear lever is quite long and protrudes from the front bulkhead.

RIGHT: **The rear-wheel-drive car's gear lever is mounted on a gearbox extension and protrudes through the transmission tunnel. The overdrive switch (when fitted) was mounted in the gear-lever knob.**

BELOW: **The engines of all the family were fitted to a separate sub-frame. This was rubber-mounted to the body shell, isolating the engine and transmission from the cabin.**

on each side using a metalastic bush. All in all, the 1300's body shell was a state-of-the-art monocoque, which utilized Triumph's expertise, both in producing a strong stiff body shell and in ensuring extensive isolation using rubber bushes for the drive train and suspension. The combination provided a degree of refinement that was not found in other manufacturers' cars.

The 1300's body shell formed the basis for all the subsequent mid-range Triumph saloons. The first changes to the shell arrived in 1970 with the

ANATOMY OF A SPORTS SALOON – TECHNICAL DESCRIPTION OF THE DOLOMITE FAMILY

introduction of the 1500 Saloon with a long-boot front-wheel-drive body and the Toledo with a short-boot rear-wheel-drive body.

The 1500 four-door saloon replaced the 1300 and incorporated a new nose and larger boot, making the 1500 slightly longer than the 1300 at 13 ft 6in (411cm) as opposed to 12ft 11in (394cm), with most of the extra 7in (17cm) being used to lengthen the boot. This increased the boot's capacity to 13.25 cubic ft (0.38 cubic metres), a 22 per cent increase from the 1300's 11 cubic ft (0.31 cubic metres). While the new shell retained the 1300's four doors, the extended boot had a higher lip than before, and the redesigned nose had what was to become the classic Dolomite look, with a pair of small 5¾in (14.6cm) diameter headlamps on each side and between them a neat grille with a central dividing 'nose', which carried the car's badge.

The front-wheel-drive 1500 was introduced in 1970 and was the first use of the long-boot body. The 1500 was bigger and more expensive than the 1300.

The 1500's rear suspension was a simple dead-beam axle and used the same mounting points as the rear-wheel-drive cars. The extra length of the boot is noticeable in this factory shot.

ANATOMY OF A SPORTS SALOON – TECHNICAL DESCRIPTION OF THE DOLOMITE FAMILY

Underneath, the shell was modified to accept the 1500's revised rear suspension, which meant that the 1300's separate sub-frame and trailing arms were replaced by a simpler and lighter tubular dead axle. This was located with a pair of trailing arms and diagonal links, which were bolted on to the body using metalastic bushes to isolate them. The tops of the rear coil over shock absorbers were located in tunnels in the wheel arches, as on the 1300. The interior dimensions remained the same as those of the 1300 shell. The 1500 shell retained the 1300's front suspension set-up and engine-mounting sub-frame.

The short-tailed, rear-wheel-drive two-door Toledo body was introduced alongside the new long-tailed 1500 in 1970. This shell was significantly changed from the 1300, as it had two doors, a heavily modified floor pan to enable the fitment of a conventional gearbox and propeller shaft, and revised rear end to accommodate a live rear axle. This was mounted on two trailing and two semi-trailing arms, which in turn were mounted directly on to the body shell as on the 1500 body shell. This resulted in a longer gearbox cover under the dash, which was extended backwards as a transmission tunnel. This meant that the 1300's flat floor and associated passenger room was lost. It also gained the new 'Dolomite' front but retained the 1300's short boot. The location of the rear suspension and axle was identical geometrically to the 1500's dead-beam system, reducing the need for different body jigs. The two-door Toledo shell was complemented by a four-door Toledo shell in 1971, which shared its doors and cabin with the long-tailed body, but retained the short boot.

The long-tail rear-wheel-drive body was the final derivative of the 1300's shell. It combined the four doors and long boot seen on the front-wheel-drive 1500 and the modified floor and live rear axle of

The rear-wheel-drive Toledo, introduced with the 1500 in 1970, used the 1300's short boot and the 1500's longer nose. The Toledo was initially offered only as a two-door body, and was a direct replacement for the 1300.

ANATOMY OF A SPORTS SALOON – TECHNICAL DESCRIPTION OF THE DOLOMITE FAMILY   39

The four-door Toledo was introduced alongside the two-door in August 1971, and used the same door size and structure as the rest of the range.

BELOW: **The four-door Toledo was in appearance very similar to the 1300. Only the new front end marked it out as a different design.**

DOLOMITE BODY SHELL TYPES

Body Type	Drive	Dates	Models
Four-door, short boot, original nose	Front-wheel drive	1966–1970	1300, 1300 TC
Four-door, long boot, Dolomite nose	Front-wheel drive	1970–1973	1500
Two-door, short boot, Dolomite nose	Rear-wheel drive	1970–1976	Toledo
Four-door, short boot, Dolomite nose	Rear-wheel drive	1971–1976	Toledo
Four-door, long boot, Dolomite nose	Rear-wheel drive	1972–80	1500 TC, Sprint, All Dolomites

the two-door Toledo to give rear-wheel drive. This shell was used on the 1500 TC and the Dolomite, along with the Sprint and the Dolomite 1300, 1500 and 1500 HL. The Dolomite's ranges of body shell had certainly undergone a somewhat convoluted evolution.

PRODUCTION OF THE DOLOMITE FAMILY BODY SHELL

The 1300's body shell was produced at Triumph's factory in Speke (the Liverpool No. 1 plant). All the steel panels were pressed there, and the shell was then welded together. After the build the body was transported to Canley, where it was painted and trimmed and had the mechanical components installed. This arrangement continued with the 1500 and Dolomites. When it was introduced, in 1970, the Toledo was built entirely at Speke – the first complete car model to be produced in its entirety at Triumph's new Liverpool No. 2 plant – but its production line was transferred to Coventry at the end of 1974 to make way for the production of the TR7.

There were a few body-shell developments that did not make it into production. An estate version of the four-door 1300 shell was mooted, and a mock-up developed, but the design was not adopted for production.

In the early 1970s the development of a two-door 'long-tail' rear-wheel-drive body shell was considered, which would have been stiffer and

The 1300 production line at the Canley plant in the 1960s. The 1300 shared the line with the 2000 model – note the 2000 Estate on the left.

While the 1300 was offered only in four-door form, the factory did experiment with the design of an estate version.

lighter than the four-door. It was planned to be marketed as a 'Toledo TS', equipped with the 1500cc twin-carb engine later seen in the 1500 TC. This shell could have given the Dolomite 1850 and Sprint variants even more performance and better handling; however, while design studies were carried out, the concept never made it into production.

At the time when the Dolomite's shell was produced, Triumph probably led the way in the UK in rust-proofing. In a 1977 Dolomite *Product Guide*, aimed at the salespeople in the dealerships, Triumph devoted a whole section to the subject – by then, the issue of rust in cars was in the public's eye. The guide gave a rundown of the processes used to protect the shell:

> *The surface areas of vulnerable joints in the box sections, wheel arches and door frames are treated with a zinc rich primer before spot welding.*
>
> *When the body is built it is thoroughly cleaned with an alkali-based cleaner to prepare it for the painting process.*
>
> *Zinc phosphate is applied to the body to provide a suitable surface for the rust protection treatment as well as providing a key for the subsequent coats of paint.*
>
> *The electrophoretic primer treatment follows when the body is immersed in a tank where the paint is attracted to it by an electric charge. This ensures that all surfaces are given a full coverage of primer.*
>
> *After checking the surface for imperfections and rectifying where necessary, a primer surface is applied to the body which is then subjected to a baking process.*
>
> *The two finishing colour coats are applied in strong synthetic alkyd enamel and then the body undergoes a final baking process.*

Once the body had been painted, the front wheel arches were fitted with plastic liners to stop the build-up of mud and the under-body and engine compartment were given a tectyl oil-based spray as a final protective coat.

All in all, this was a very thorough rust-proofing process, and probably contributed to the survival of many Triumphs to this day. In addition to the factory treatment, the Ziebart company offered through the dealer network an additional rust-proofing service (costing around £38 in the early 1970s, when a Dolomite cost around £1,400 on the road). This involved injecting a wax solution into the box sections, sills and other vulnerable parts of the body shell. The Ziebart process left a number of small bungs in the body shell, most obviously on the rear door shuts; at least two of the Dolomites featured in this book bear the evidence of having had the treatment.

ANATOMY OF A SPORTS SALOON – TECHNICAL DESCRIPTION OF THE DOLOMITE FAMILY

Many Triumphs from the 1970s had the aftermarket Ziebart anti-rust treatment, which was often done by the selling dealer. Rubber plugs giving access to the box sections are evidence that the treatment has been done.

THE POWER BEHIND THE 1300 AND 1500

The 1300's engine was the only part of the car that was not all new. It was actually based on the Standard 'SC' (for 'small car') unit, which originally appeared as an 803cc straight four in 1953 powering Standard's small four-door saloon cars, the Eight, Ten and Pennant. The new small Standard saloon was designed to meet the threat of the Austin A30 and the Morris Minor, and its 803cc engine and associated four-speed gearbox was to compete directly with the then new BMC A-Series small engine. While the Standard engine was all new, there was a particular constraint placed on the design: because Canley had recently been re-equipped with the machine tools to bore and hone the engine blocks for the 1247cc Mayflower (which was now defunct), the Standard

The first of the Dolomite family fitted with the 'SC' engine in conventional rear-wheel-drive format was the Toledo. The engine also served in this form in the 1500 TC, Dolomite 1300 and Dolomite 1500.

engine was required to re-use the same cylinder centres. Like the A-series the Standard engine was an in-line four-cylinder, overhead-valve unit with a capacity of 803cc, with a three main bearing crankshaft and bore and stroke of 58 x 76mm. However, apart from sharing the bore and stroke, the Standard engine was very different from the A-series, not least in its development potential, which allowed the capacity to be increased to 1493cc. It was in this guise that it would replace the A-series in the MG Midget 1500 model.

Designed by a small team headed by talented engineer David Eley, a lifelong Standard employee, the engine was reasonably compact, with a cast-iron block and cylinder head, and a pressed-steel sump. The overall layout of the engine was conventional for the time: inlet and exhaust manifolds on the right-hand side, a chain-driven camshaft on the opposite side to the manifolds, and pushrod-operated overhead valves. The chain drive for the camshaft was taken from the nose of the crankshaft, and the chain and sprockets were situated in a pressed-steel chain case on the front of the crankcase. The cylinder head had four separate exhaust ports, to give better breathing – unlike the A-series, which had only three – and a pair of siamezed inlet

Capacity	Bore and stroke (mm)	Power	Torque	Comp. ratio	Notes	Model
803cc	58 x 76	26bhp @ 4,500rpm	NA	7:1	Single carb	Standard 8
948cc	63 x 76	35bhp @ 4,500rpm	51lb ft at 2,750rpm	8:1	Single carb	Standard 10, Herald
948cc	63 x 76	45bhp @ 6,000rpm	51lb ft at 4,200rpm	8.5:1	Twin carb	Herald Coupé
1147cc	69.3 x 76	39bhp @ 4,500rpm	61lb ft at 2,250rpm	8:1	Single carb	Herald 12/50
1147cc	69.3 x 76	63bhp @ 5,750rpm	67lb ft at 3,500rpm	9:1	Twin carb	Spitfire Mk 1
1147cc	69.3 x 76	67bhp @ 6,000rpm	67lb ft at 3,750rpm	9:1	Twin carb	Spitfire Mk 2
1296cc	73.7 x 76	61bhp @ 5,000rpm	73lb ft at 4,200rpm	8.5:1	Single carb	Herald 13/60, 1300
1296cc	73.7 x 76	75bhp @ 6.000rpm (DIN)	75lb ft at 4,000rpm	9:1	Twin carb	Spitfire Mk 3, 1300 TC
1296cc	73.7 x 76	63bhp @ 6,000rpm	69lb ft at 3,500rpm	9:1	Twin carb	Spitfire Mk 4
1296cc	73.7 x 76	58bhp @ 6,000rpm (DIN)	70lb ft at 3,000rpm	8.5:1	Single carb	Toledo, Dolomite 1300
1493cc	73.7 x 87.5	61bhp @ 5,000rpm (DIN)	81lb ft at 2,700rpm	8.5:1	Single carb	1500 (up to Oct 1971)
1493cc	73.7 x 87.5	65bhp @ 5,000rpm (DIN))	80lb ft at 3,000rpm	9.0:1	Single carb	1500 (from Oct 1971)
1493cc	73.7 x 87.5	71bhp @ 5,500rpm (DIN)	82lb ft at 3,000rpm	9.0:1	Twin carb	Spitfire 1500
1493cc	73.7 x 87.5	64bhp @ 5,000rpm (DIN)	78lb ft at 3,000rpm	8.5:1	Twin carb	1500 TC, Dolomite 1500

ports. Internally, there were three main bearings, a steel crankshaft and con rods, and alloy pistons. The engine was not like the larger post-war Standard unit, which had wet liners – on the new engine, the cylinder bores were part of the block casting and the block had water passages cast in. All the ancillaries (dynamo, oil filter, distributor, starter motor and spark plugs) were positioned on the camshaft (left) side of the engine, making for a very neat and tidy unit. The camshaft was used to drive the distributor and oil pump from a spur drive. The water pump and thermostat were housed in a separate casting, which was bolted to the front of the engine, and the pump was powered by a belt that also drove the dynamo and engine-cooling fan.

The engine was also originally designed to be bored out to 63mm, to give a capacity of 948cc. In this guise the engine lost its water channels between the front two and rear two cylinders, to allow for the larger bores. The engine appeared in the Standard Eight of 1953 in 803cc guise, and in 1954 its 948cc derivative appeared in the Standard Ten. The engine was first used in a Triumph (apart from the TR10 Saloon and estate car, a re-badged Standard Ten marketed only in the USA) in the Herald in 1959, where it powered the new small saloon in 948cc guise. The engine's capacity was raised to 1147cc by increasing the bore to 69.3mm for 1961, and this version powered the Herald 1200 series through to 1970.

DEVELOPMENT OF THE STANDARD TRIUMPH 'SC' ENGINE

Despite having a three main bearing crankshaft throughout its long life, the SC family of engines could be reliably tuned to produce power outputs that were quite outstanding for the day. The works Spitfires for 1965 with 1147cc units produced up to 109bhp, while the engine's ultimate incarnation came with the works Spitfire rally cars used in the 1965 Alpine Rally. These, with their eight-port cylinder heads and capacity of 1296cc, reliably produced 117bhp – quite a leap from the original 803cc unit's 26bhp.

After the stretch to 1147cc the next step was to take the engine capacity out to 1296cc by increasing the bore to the maximum 73.7mm. This engine, usually referred to as the Triumph 1300 unit, was the first power plant used in the Dolomite range, powering the original 1300 saloon and the Herald 13/60. In this guise, the engine had a single carburettor and gave a respectable 61bhp.

The main consideration in terms of accommodating the 1300's front-wheel-drive configuration was the positioning of the starter motor. On the conventional rear-wheel-drive units the starter drove a ring gear on the flywheel at the rear of the engine. The 1300's front-wheel-drive system had the gearbox bolted to the bottom of the block. This meant that drive was taken from the rear of the clutch by a set of step-down gears. This configuration meant that the starter motor had to be placed at the front of the engine and drove an exposed starter ring that was mounted on the nose of the crankshaft. The engine's sump was formed in the top of the bolt-on transmission casting, so the engine could be lifted out without having to disturb the transmission.

The final stretch of the SC engine was a further increase in bore to 87.5mm, which, with the 1296cc unit's stroke of 87.5mm, gave a capacity of 1493cc. The new capacity gave only a slight increase in power over the 1296cc variant, but it did a significant boost to the torque of the unit which significantly improved the performance of the 1500 saloons.

MORE POWER – 1850 SLANT FOUR

The 1972 Dolomite was the first Triumph car to receive the company's new slant four engine, but it was not the first car to use it; that honour went to the Saab 99 of 1968. The slant four unit's history went back to 1963, when an internal study carried out by Triumph's engineering facility and led by Lewis Dawtrey was convened to determine Triumph's future engine strategy. While they had the Standard-derived SC unit at the lower end, and the straight six-cylinder engine in 1600cc and 2000cc (with scope to grow to 2500cc) capacities,

ANATOMY OF A SPORTS SALOON – TECHNICAL DESCRIPTION OF THE DOLOMITE FAMILY

it was felt that a new, modern range of engines was needed – preferably one that could provide a family of power units from 1500cc up to 3000cc. The result was a four-cylinder in-line unit, which could be built in 1500cc to 2000cc capacities and a V8, which in prototype form was a 2500cc unit and which was finally produced as a full 3000cc for the Stag. In order for the design to be suitable as a straight four or a V8, the 4-cylinder design had its cylinders canted over by 45 degrees.

This gave the 4-cylinder engine design much in common with the V8 version, and also allowed for a lower (but wider) engine, facilitating a lower bonnet line. This was common practice among a number of other car manufacturers at the time, most notably Lotus with its 2-litre double overhead-cam, 16-valve unit and Vauxhall's 2-litre (later 2.3) unit. The study determined that the new four-cylinder engine should feature a cast-iron one-piece cylinder block, a light alloy cylinder head, a chain-driven single overhead camshaft operating two valves per cylinder, either a carburettor or mechanical fuel injection and a chain-driven jack shaft running the length of the engine, supported on four bearings. The jack shaft was originally intended to provide a drive for the distributor, oil pump and the proposed fuel-injection metering unit, and the water pump was originally to be placed in a casting on the front of the engine and was to be belt-driven from the crankshaft pulley. The distributor and fuel-injection unit were both to be mounted on top of the engine and the oil pump was mounted below the distributor; all were driven from skew gears on the shaft, with a shared drive at the rear of the engine for the distributor and oil pump, and a second drive towards the front for the fuel-injection unit.

The use of an overhead camshaft was quite rare in the British motor industry at the time and was usually limited to more exotic British performance engines. Continental competitors, such as Fiat, BMW and Alfa Romeo, did offer several overhead or even double overhead-cam units. However, the use of an overhead cam on the new Triumph unit was not intended to gain ultimate performance. Instead, Triumph's philosophy on the use of an overhead camshaft was slightly different, as discussed by Harry Webster and Spen King in an interview with George Bulmer of *Motor* magazine in June 1968.

The Dolomite 1850 engine was a comfortable fit in the Dolomite engine bay. Access to the distributor and water pump was awkward as they lived underneath the inlet manifold.

The Dolomite's engine was a 45-degree slant four. The overhead cam lived under a pressed-steel cover with the oil filler cap at the front and 'TRIUMPH' embossed into the pressing.

According to the Triumph engineers, while the use of an overhead camshaft did not offer any weight saving over a pushrod design, it did allow them to get better porting within a given length of engine. It also enabled the use of bigger valves, made for a better casting design and allowed for more radical valve timing. The designers could be more brutal with the valve opening and closing than they could with a pushrod design and this gave better low-down torque for the same top-end power.

While the new Triumph unit was being designed, Swedish manufacturer Saab was working with British engineering consultancy firm Ricardo to design a new four-stroke four-cylinder engine for its 99 model. When it realized that Triumph was developing a similar engine, Ricardo pointed Saab in Triumph's direction. As a result, Saab used a Triumph-built 1708cc version of the engine, designated PE 104S, in its 99 from 1968, with an 1854cc unit being adopted by the Swedes from early in 1971.

Following some reliability issues with the Triumph-built engines, Saab took over design responsibility and manufacture of its own versions of the unit during 1972. In 1978 Saab introduced the 99 Turbo model with 145bhp, delivering reliable turbocharger technology to the mass market. The use of a turbo meant that Saab could gain a significant power boost from what was by then its four-cylinder motor for very little extra cost and weight – and of course it could still charge a premium price for its cars. Those Saab Turbo models are now considered to be legendary, thanks to their superior performance. The Saab-designed turbo unit, along with the Dolomite Sprint unit, were the ultimate developments of the original Triumph slant four unit.

The Dolomite's version of the slant four engine had a cast-iron block, aluminium head and chain-driven overhead cam, with five plain main bearings and plain big ends on split connecting rods. The pistons were alloy, and were fitted with three piston rings, two compression and one oil scraper. The valves were in line, and were operated directly from the camshaft using buckets with cast-iron valve seats and valve guides.

The camshaft and ancillary drive shaft was driven by a single-row $3/8$-inch width chain driven from a sprocket on the crankshaft nose, and the lower half of the drive train was housed in a cast-alloy timing case. While Triumph's original design for the four-cylinder unit had a conventional water

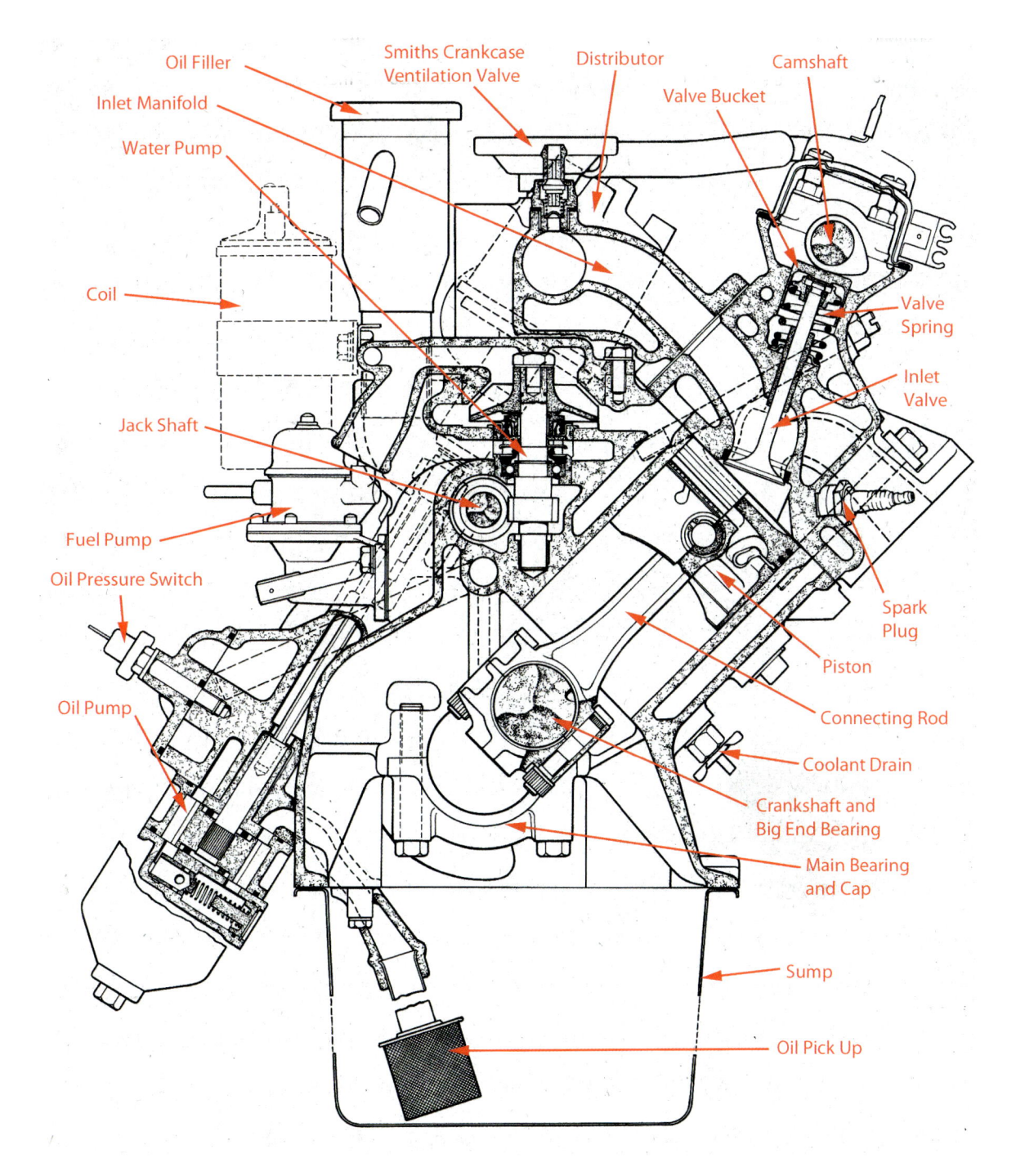

The Dolomite engine was designed to take up minimal height in the engine bay, hence its 45-degree slant. The design also lent itself to a V8 that was used in the Triumph Stag.

pump mounted on the front of the unit, Saab intended to use the engine as a front-wheel-drive unit, with the gearbox under the engine. However, Saab did not want to redesign its existing gearbox, which was configured to take its drive from the front of the engine. As a result, the new Triumph engine had to be turned through 180 degrees in the Saab engine bay, so that the clutch and flywheel

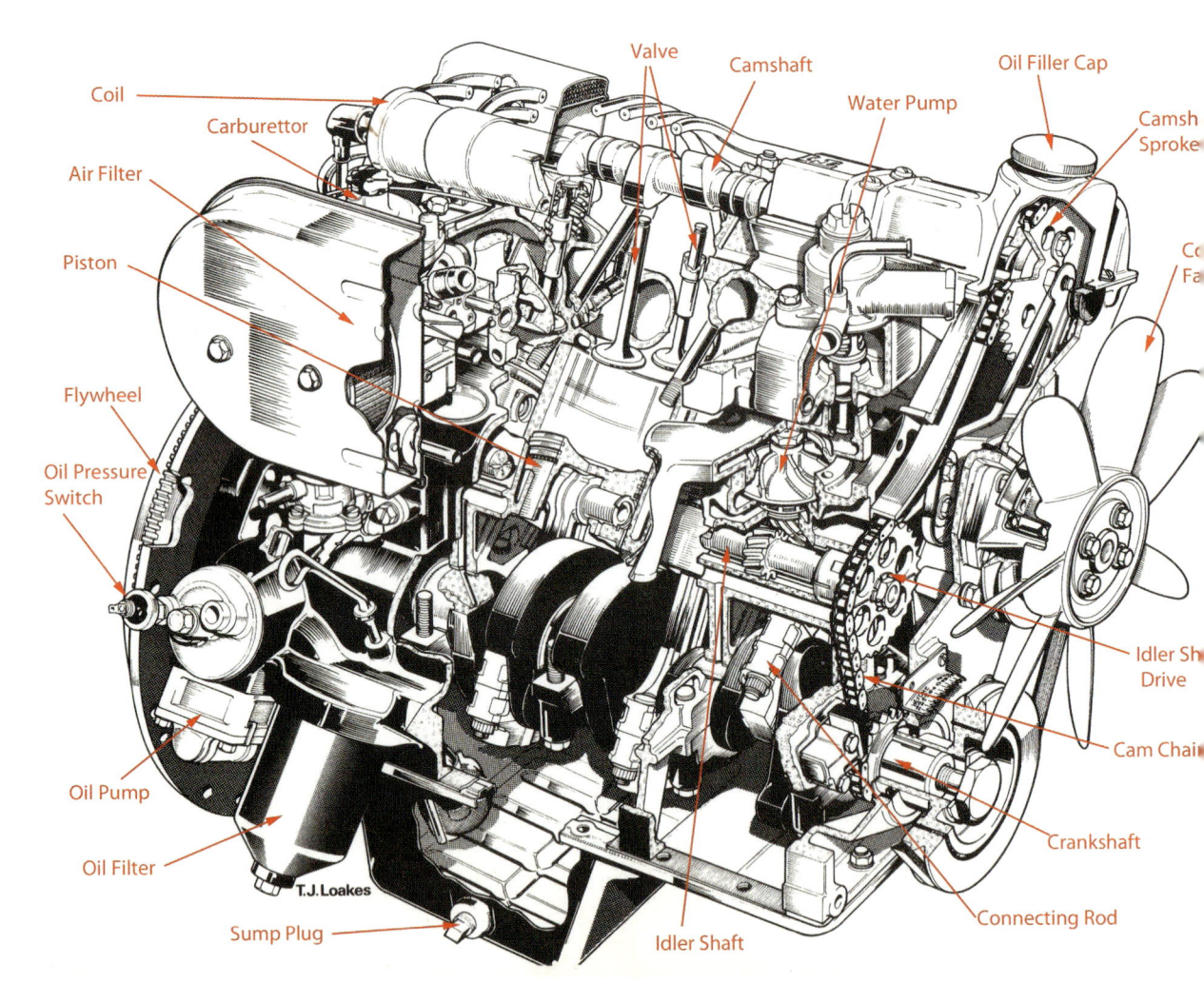

48 ■ ANATOMY OF A SPORTS SALOON – TECHNICAL DESCRIPTION OF THE DOLOMITE FAMILY

The Dolomite engine had an ancillary shaft to drive the water pump and distributor and oil pump, and a chain-driven overhead camshaft that operated the valve directly.

faced forwards – otherwise the new Saab would have had one forward and four reverse gears. This reorientation meant that the position of the water pump on the front of the unit was untenable – with the engine turned round there was not enough space for the water pump to be sited between what had now become the rear of the block and the Saab's bulkhead. There was no easy way to provide a separate drive for the pump at the flywheel end of the motor, so the pump was repositioned on the top of the cylinder block. It was then driven by the spur gear on the ancillary drive shaft originally intended to drive the fuel-injection metering unit, which was redundant as Saab was proposing to use a carburettor. With the water pump positioned on the top of the crankcase in a coolant gallery, the water pump impeller itself was sealed from the drive mechanism on the ancillary shaft with a graphite seal. Towards the back of the engine the AC Delco distributor had centrifugal and vacuum advance mechanisms and housed the contact breaker points.

The Dolomite's cylinder head was cast in alloy and had wedge-shaped combustion chambers. The valve guides were pressed in and the steel valve seats were cast in place. The eight valves

ANATOMY OF A SPORTS SALOON – TECHNICAL DESCRIPTION OF THE DOLOMITE FAMILY

LEFT: **The Dolomite Sprint engine had a duplex chain driving the camshaft. The flat-topped pistons, water pump and camshaft drive sprocket are visible in this shot.**

BELOW: **At the front of Dolomite engine there was an alloy timing cover that housed the cam chain. The pulley for the belt-driven viscous fan coupling are visible.**

(two per cylinder) were placed in a line and driven directly from the single camshaft through buckets and shims, while the head was line-bored to allow the cam to be carried in five split bearings, held in place by caps. A pressed-steel cam cover, with 'Triumph' pressed into it in large text, finished off the top end of the motor. With twin carburettors and a 9.0 to 1 compression ratio, when fitted to the Dolomite 1850 in 1972, the engine produced a healthy 91bhp at 5,200rpm and, more significantly, 105lb ft of torque at 3,500rpm. This gave the car great driveability, along with a 100mph (160km/h) top speed and a 0–60mph time of 11.3 seconds.

When the slant four was first exposed to the press there was universal acclaim. In its first test of the Dolomite, *Motor* magazine (8 January 1972) described the engine as 'torquey and effortless' and as being 'by far and away the best "four" in BL's armoury'. The opinion of *Autocar* following its test (6 January 1972) was that the Dolomite's engine 'must rate as one of the smoothest and most refined fours we have ever experienced'. Unfortunately, despite the plaudits from the press and the undoubted quality of the Triumph engine, the only other production Triumph (or indeed British Leyland) car to use the slant four was the Triumph TR7, which had a bored-out 2-litre version of the eight-valve unit.

MICHAEL A. SOUBRY'S 'YELLOW BIRD'

Michael Soubry is the proud owner of a 1972 Triumph Dolomite that he has owned from new. He was born in 1940, and in 1972, after a stint working abroad on a civil engineering project in Pakistan, he was returning to the UK. Having sold his Alfa Romeo Giulia TI, he needed to buy a new car. He had his mother send him brochures from a number of manufacturers, and chose the Dolomite as the one to have from a shortlist of small sporting saloons, including the BMW 2002 Touring and the Fiat 125. As well as being British, the Dolomite offered much better equipment levels than the German contender, and did not have the 'rust-bucket' reputation that Fiats had acquired in the UK.

Ordering the new Triumph Dolomite from a British Leyland main dealer in central London, Michael picked the car up in July 1972, with a 'K' registration – the dealer could not understand why he did not wait until August, to give the car an 'L' registration! At the time, UK registration numbers were age-related with the format ABC123D; the final letter denoted the year, which changed on the first of August. The timing of the letter change was intended to stimulate sales at a traditionally quiet time of the sales year. The 'new year' letters were eagerly awaited by many new car buyers and not just in a spirit of one-upmanship. As the letter clearly denoted a car's age, it had a disproportionate influence on that car's second-hand value. Of course, the dealer had Michael's best interests at heart when he tried to persuade him to wait until August, when the 'L' registration would be introduced, but he could not have realized that his customer had no intention of selling the car after a couple of years. In fact, he still owns it over 42 years later!

The car is a 1972 manual in Saffron (Triumph colour no. 54), with black trim and a manual gearbox. The only option available at the time was an automatic gearbox; much to Michael's regret, there was no overdrive option at the model's introduction. What he did like about

All the cars in the Dolomite family had opening front quarter lights and manual windows. Despite his height, Michael Soubry finds his Dolomite very comfortable.

the car, apart from its overall performance and accommodation, was the little touches that made living with the car easy. These included the standard inertia reel seatbelts with their 'cassette'-type latch on the transmission tunnel, which were very easy to use; the mounting points for rear seatbelts which he used to fit harnesses for his children; and the servo-assisted brakes that provided the car with the stopping power commensurate with the car's performance. The car's handy size and its manoeuvrability made it easy to drive and park back in the 1970s. Still using it as his daily driver, Michael finds these benefits even more relevant in a time of shrinking parking spaces and ever larger cars. A colleague of Michael's christened the car 'Yellow Bird' when he first saw it and Michael adopted the name and has used it ever since.

Owning the car from new, Michael has had some problems. Back in the dark days of British Leyland, customer service in some dealerships had declined to medieval levels and the concept of after-sales service was completely alien. The dealer from whom Michael bought the Dolomite refused to do anything about the first problem he encountered, which was a faulty gearbox, despite the car being under guarantee. It was only after changing to another dealer that the fault was fixed with a gearbox rebuild and some new cogs.

The only other irritating problem was the failure of the electric screen-washer pump. When Michael bought the Dolomite, UK law had recently changed to prohibit hand-operated screen-wash systems on new cars. When Michael's pump failed there were no spares available in the country for some months, so, through no fault of his own, he had to drive the car in an illegal state. (Interestingly, my uncle bought a new Austin Allegro at around the same time. His electric washer pump also failed and he was unable to acquire a replacement for months. When it finally arrived, it was found to be made in Japan, which caused some ironic smiles.)

Poor customer service was a feature of virtually every service in the first three decades of ownership, as Michael recalls:

> The screw for tightening the contact breaker points after re-setting their gap is difficult to get to in the middle of the top of the engine. To the family's dismay, immediately after any service operation I used to ensure I carried a handy screwdriver with me ready for the almost-inevitable breakdown. I would splutter to the side of the road, hop out and re-set the points and tighten them (securely this time) and off we would go again.

From new, Michael fitted 'Desmo' wing mirrors, which he still prefers to the door mirrors seen on all modern cars. They were superior to the fixed items that Triumph offered as an extra as they were spring-back items, so a minor knock did not put them out of adjustment. He drilled the front wings and made sure he protected the paintwork around the holes when he fitted them. After buying the car, he found that the front end felt light at speed, so, after some correspondence with the Rover Triumph Service department, he bought and fitted a Dolomite chin spoiler that BL had made available. This improved the situation no end. The car's handling and road-holding are good, but early on Michael had a hairy moment going round a left-hand corner at speed:

> I took to the road on my familiar commuting rat-run only to do a sharp left turn that left me 'fighting the wheel' to regain control. While other aspects of my previous Alfa were inferior to the Dolomite, the Alfa went round every corner at every speed as though on rails, had, figuratively, 'saved' me on several occasions, and clearly had led me into a dangerous over-confidence on cornering.

The boot of the Dolomite is a reasonable size, although it was considered at the time of manufacture to be a bit shallow. The standard jack and tool kit along with its plastic bag are still present in Michael's car.

continued overleaf

MICHAEL A. SOUBRY'S 'YELLOW BIRD' continued

The black highlights on the 'C' pillars and the rear panel marked the Dolomite out as something special.

Michael's Dolomite sits square to the road and is in great condition.

Other than that hiccup, the Dolomite has not disappointed him, and he finds its precise and direct steering gives him plenty of confidence to slice through traffic. He finds the back end can be a bit skittish in the wet, and always fits tyres with good wet-weather grip; he originally used Dunlop SP Sports with Aquajets, and today uses Goodyear Grand Prix Ss. As he ran the car through the 1980s he found the mild-steel exhaust needed more and more frequent repairs and the replacement parts were pretty poor quality. This led him in 1989 to the 'London Stainless Steel Exhaust Centre' where he bought a full stainless system, parts of which are still on the car today.

In the same year, at around 90,000 miles, the original engine was suffering from a number of oil and water leaks. Michael put it in for a rebuild, but galvanic corrosion had firmly welded the cylinder-head studs to the head, so a reconditioned replacement engine was fitted. One strange fault that emerged in 1986 was the failure of the night dimming relay. This relay, positioned in the boot, was fitted to dim the indicators and brake lights when the lights were on, to avoid dazzling other drivers. When it failed, the lights went haywire, with Michael finding himself unable to predict what electrical equipment would function when the lights, indicators or brake lights were operated. He was unable to diagnose the fault himself, so made a visit to specialists Auto Electrical Centre. The fault was quickly traced to the night dimming relay and removal of the relay fixed the problem.

By the 1990s the driver's seat had become a bit threadbare, so Michael replaced both front seats with a pair of second-hand items from a later Dolomite that had the built-in head restraints – a safety feature that Michael appreciates to this day. The original 15in (37.5cm) diameter steering wheel was replaced when the leather stitching failed, and a slightly smaller 14in (35cm) Moto-Lita item was fitted on the recommendation of Rimmer Bros. While he was worried that the smaller diameter would make the unassisted steering even heavier when parking, Michael could not feel any difference and it had the bonus of giving him more room for his thighs under the wheel.

The only other major upgrade Michael has made to the car is the fitting of electronic ignition. The Lumenition Optronic system has proved to be a true fit-and-forget option and he no longer has to carry a screwdriver to re-adjust the points after every service.

Performance-wise, Michael finds the car good. He has seen 100–105mph (160–170km/h) on the speedometer, and the car will cruise happily at 90–95mph (145–155km/h) on the autobahn. The

A small 'DOLOMITE' badge on the grille and a 'TRIUMPH' badge on the top of the front panel identify the car, along with the trademark twin headlamps and black grille.

continued overleaf

MICHAEL A. SOUBRY'S 'YELLOW BIRD' continued

Under the bonnet Michael's Dolomite is standard. Note the preservative wax still on the inner wings.

car's best point is its mid-range acceleration, from 30mph to 50mph (48 to 80km/h), which was class-beating in its day at under 8 seconds and still pretty respectable today. A trip up the motorway to Birmingham with his boss in the 1970s confirmed that the car's ride was more comfortable than that of a Triumph 2000. On the negative side he does find the car somewhat noisy – much of it wind noise – especially in comparison with modern cars. The only time the car has let his family down was in the early hours of one morning when his wife and daughter were driving to Leicester and the throttle cable broke.

By 2006, although the Dolomite was looking a bit tired, Michael's daughter Caroline wanted to use it as the transport to her wedding. The body had survived the years well, but a few cosmetic issues were spoiling the look of the car, so a spruce-up was needed. Michael approached Abinger Hammer Motors, the Triumph specialist in Surrey who had been servicing the car for a few years. As Michael recalls, they concentrated on the bodywork, with a really good partial re-spray in the original Triumph Saffron:

As the wedding of my daughter approached we realized that in her lifetime she had known only the Triumph as the family car, any others having been company cars. This seemed like an opportunity, so the de-rusting became part of the wedding project. I insisted that it was not to be a complete re-spray so that some of the original Saffron paint colour would remain. Abinger Hammer accepted the challenge and did a great job with the paint match.

Following the refresh, I drove Caroline (and her bridesmaid) to the church. The groom provided the transport to whisk her away after the ceremony, so an end of an era would be complete. The day of the wedding was very hot. On the way to the church we stopped at a garage to buy a bottle of water for the bridesmaid. The second transport Daimler Landaulet heading for the wedding venue was passing at the time and touchingly (and untrustingly) swept in too, concerned that we might be in mechanical trouble. Caroline particularly appreciated the historical absence of seat belts in the back of the Dolomite to allow her greater comfort for the journey and her wedding dress to remain unspoilt.

What a way to complete over four decades of ownership of a brilliant car!

ANATOMY OF A SPORTS SALOON – TECHNICAL DESCRIPTION OF THE DOLOMITE FAMILY

Inside, a Moto-Lita steering wheel is the only departure from standard.

BELOW: **When his daughter Caroline was married, Michael found that the Dolomite made an ideal wedding car. (Thanks to Michael A. Soubry)**

YET MORE POWER – THE SPRINT

Once the Dolomite's slant four engine was finalized, Triumph's chief engineer Spen King was tasked to develop a high-performance version of the unit with an eye to competition work. The objective was to achieve a significant increase in power over the standard engine. King now had significant engineering skills available to him in the British Leyland organization, including the famous engineer Walter Hassan, who was working for

Jaguar at the time and chaired the British Leyland group that concentrated on future engine policy. In his autobiography, *Climax in Coventry*, Hassan relates how he and Harry Mundy (another talented Jaguar engineer who had designed, among other projects, the Lotus Elan's twin-cam engine cylinder head) discussed and passed on data about four-valve cylinder heads to Spen King. He also emphasized the fact that he had no input to the actual design of the engine and was full of admiration for the fine job achieved by Spen King and his team with the Sprint engine.

The advantages of four valves were clear; not only did they increase the overall area of the port, allowing more gas to flow, the smaller valve sizes also encouraged faster gas flow. The smaller valves were individually lighter than a single valve used in a two-valve head, so had less inertia and could be opened and closed much faster, again encouraging greater gas flow into and out of the engine.

Lewis Dawtry, the original architect of the slant four and V8 Triumph units, was responsible for the detail design of the high-performance motor. Four valves per cylinder was agreed on as being the best way forward – no doubt partly spurred on by the Ford BDA engine introduced in 1969 and the Lotus 900 series engines first seen in the Jensen Healey of 1972. However, the width and complexity of a twin-cam head was less than desirable, especially as its width would raise the height of the slant four engine and obscure the water pump and distributor on the top of the block.

On many double overhead-camshaft engines the two camshafts are identical, sharing the same profile and giving the same valve timing and lift for inlet and exhaust valves. The actual gas flow into such an engine was dependent on the size of the valves and the shaping of the ports. Engines using the same camshaft profiles for inlet and exhaust included the original Lotus Twin Cam engine, and the Lotus 900 series sixteen-valve unit. In these twin-camshaft engines, the common practice was to have the cam lobes acting directly on the valve stems, cutting down parts and producing an efficient engine that was relatively simple to manufacture. Valve adjustment was usually achieved using shims between the cam lobe and the valve stem. While this system was fiddly to set up initially, it did tend to stay in adjustment longer than the more conventional tappet and lock-nut method used on rockers.

If a single overhead camshaft was used, the valves could be operated in two ways, which would influence the design of the combustion chamber. Many

Under the bonnet the Sprint engine is recognizable by its large cam cover, usually painted black.

ANATOMY OF A SPORTS SALOON – TECHNICAL DESCRIPTION OF THE DOLOMITE FAMILY   57

While the cylinder head of the Sprint was wider than the 'standard' 1850 unit, the extra width was concentrated on the lower side of the head, so the engine actually took up very little extra space.

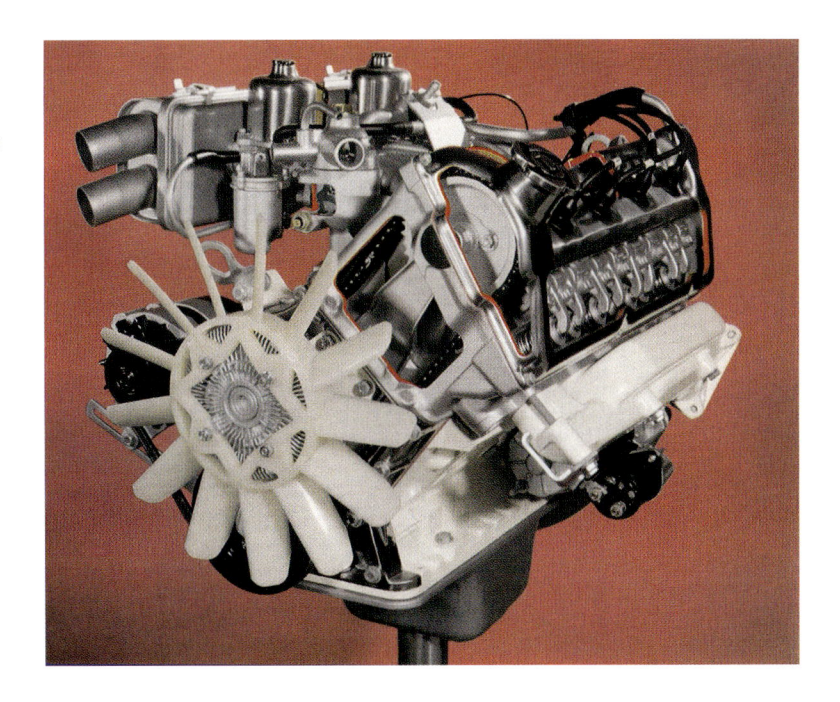

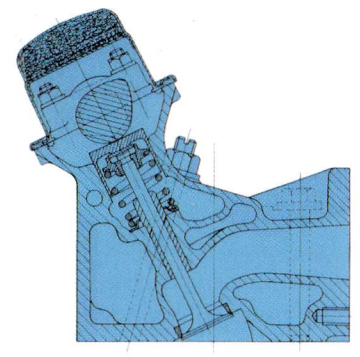

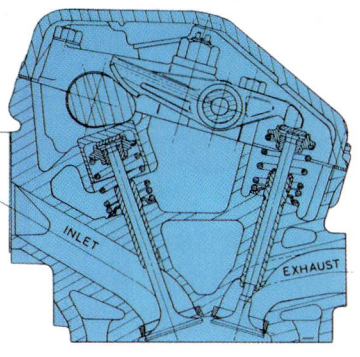

The Sprint engine was a sophisticated unit and the first mass-production engine with four valves per cylinder. Top left shows the camshaft drive and rockers. The lower left is a cross-section of the standard Dolomite head, and the lower right is the Sprint.

The Sprint engine's valve gear was a clever design that won a Design Council award. Visible here is the wider duplex chain used to drive the camshaft.

engines, including the existing Triumph slant four as used on the Dolomite 1850, had their valves in a line along the axis of the engine, with the camshaft lobes operating directly on the valve stems. This method resulted in a wedge-shaped combustion chamber, which was good for torque but not so good for ultimate power. It was relatively easy to manufacture although the initial set-up of the valve clearances using shims was fiddly. The second method was to use a central camshaft with rockers to operate both the inlet and exhaust valves. This method was used extensively by Honda in its car and motorbike engines, and enabled the use of a hemispherical combustion chamber, which, at the time, was the optimum form for high power. Such an engine was relatively easy to manufacture, but had the disadvantage of more moving parts (the rockers, associated shafts and valve adjusters) and more weight and inertia in the valve system than the inline valve configuration.

When designing the Sprint engine, the Triumph engineers managed to incorporate the best features of both these types of valve gear in an exceptionally neat and compact design, which delivered a head with an efficient combustion chamber and reliable four valves per cylinder valve train. It was easy to manufacture and could be applied to the existing Triumph slant four engine with minimal engineering changes.

The Sprint's cylinder head was cast in light alloy and the design resulted in a single camshaft head with sixteen valves, which, while larger than the standard engine's eight-valve head, was not as bulky as a twin-camshaft head would have been. The camshaft had eight lobes and was driven from the nose of the crank using a duplex chain; a hydraulic tensioner maintained the correct tension and the whole drive assembly was encased in an alloy timing cover that bolted to the front of the block, the head and the sump. The valves were arranged in two lines of eight; angled at 27 degrees from the vertical, with 1.38in (35.1mm) diameter inlets and smaller 1.21in (30.7mm) diameter exhaust valves. The inlet valves were operated directly from the camshaft. As the inlet valves were larger in diameter and heavier than the exhaust valves, it made

With the camshaft operating the inlet valves directly, the exhaust valves were operated by rockers.

A four-valve head enabled better gas flow in a circular combustion chamber as two smaller valves give a larger area than a larger-diameter single valve. The Sprint's cylinder head was a classic four-valve design, with the spark plug centrally positioned between the valves.

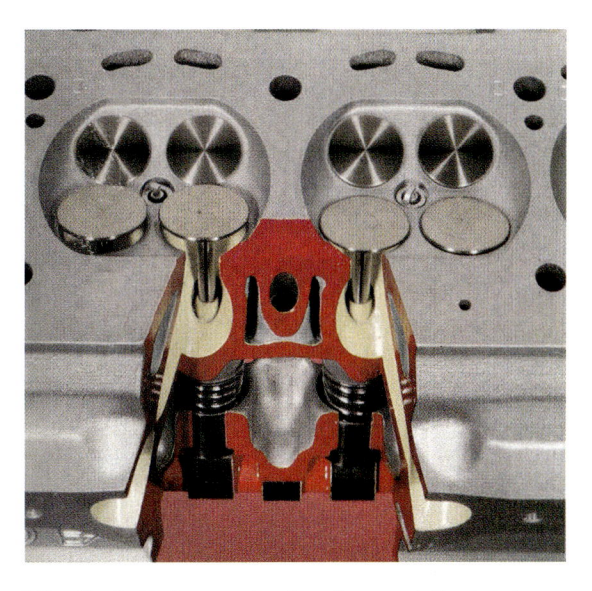

The Sprint's four-valve head meant the inlet and exhaust ports had to be siamesed to feed each valve. A lot of precision machining is needed to get the head from a bare casting to a production-ready item.

sense to use the camshaft to operate them directly, in order to minimize the inertia of the valve train. This clever design won the UK's Design Council Award for 1974.

The exhaust valves were operated by solid one-piece rockers, which pivoted on a common shaft parallel to the camshaft and were driven by the same camshaft lobes used to operate the

RELATIVE OUTPUTS OF THE THREE SLANT FOUR VARIANTS

Capacity	Bore and stroke (mm)	Power	Torque	Comp. ratio	Notes	Model
1854cc	87 × 78	91bhp (DIN) @ 5,200rpm	105lb ft at 3,500rpm	9.0:1	8-valve	Dolomite
1998cc	90.3 × 78.0	127bhp (DIN) @ 5,700rpm	122lb ft at 4,500rpm	9.5:1	16-valve	Sprint
1998cc	90.3 × 78.0	105bhp (DIN) @ 5,500rpm	119lb ft at 3,500rpm	9.25:1	8-valve	TR7 (UK)

inlet valves, with the positioning of the rockers on the cam radius determining the exhaust valve timing. As the exhaust valves were smaller and lighter than the inlets, the use of rockers to operate them with the associated increase in inertia was not as significant as if the inlets were driven by rockers. So the single camshaft was used to operate all sixteen valves, with each of the eight lobes on the camshaft operating one inlet and one exhaust valve. Valve adjustment was achieved using different sizes of shim, as on the eight-valve engine, with the shims placed on the top of the inlet and exhaust valve stems to provide correct valve clearances.

The spark plugs were perfectly positioned in the apex of the combustion chamber, each plug sitting in a detachable spark-plug tube. The cam cover was a large one-piece alloy casting, which was fixed to the periphery of the head and front chain case with six screws. The centre of the case had fixings to meet up with the spark-plug tubes to give access to the spark plugs. This system required seals between each spark-plug tube and the cylinder head and cam cover. While this was a neat solution to the problem of giving access to the spark plugs, and is commonly used today, the tubes could leak, allowing engine oil to flood the spark-plug tunnel and short out the plugs.

Apart from the cylinder head, the Sprint engine was changed only slightly from the eight-valve unit. The capacity was raised to a full 2 litres (1998cc) by boring the engine, as was allowed for in the original design. The other difference was the valve gear being driven by a duplex chain rather than the eight-valve unit's single-row chain, which required a slightly wider alloy timing cover. The ability to unbolt the camshaft drive sprocket was retained, allowing the head to be removed without affecting the valve timing. The engine was fed by a pair of SU carburettors rather than the 1850's Strombergs – as Triumph and BMC were joined by the time the Sprint was introduced, there was no need for Triumph to use its own Strombergs.

The three production uses for the slant four engine were in eight-valve, 1854cc guise in the Dolomite, the sixteen-valve 1998cc Sprint unit and the eight-valve 1998cc unit used in the TR7.

GEARBOX, TRANSMISSION AND FINAL DRIVE

The first of the family, the 1300, sported an advanced and innovative front-wheel-drive system that was radically different from the BMC Mini/1100 series front-wheel-drive system, which used a transverse engine with its gearbox in the sump and the final drive behind the engine. The Triumph boasted a longitudinal engine with a separate gearbox and final drive sitting underneath it, driven through the clutch by a set of step-down gears bolted to the back of the engine. While this increased the height of the engine/transmission unit, it also allowed for a good steering lock. (This was a legacy from the Herald, although circumstances would dictate that the turning circle of the production 1300s would not be as small as originally envisaged.) It also meant that as

ANATOMY OF A SPORTS SALOON – TECHNICAL DESCRIPTION OF THE DOLOMITE FAMILY

much of the weight of the unit as possible was kept behind the front wheels, for good weight distribution, and that the engine, gearbox and transmission oil were not shared. The latter was a particular bugbear of Harry Webster, who was a great advocate of using the correctly formulated oil in the right places. It had also been found that most engine noise emanated from the sides of the block; Triumph's longitudinal positioning of the engine meant there was less engine noise to intrude into the cabin.

Just visible in this shot of the 1300's engine bay is the differential output under the engine and the flexible rubber 'donut' used to allow the driveshaft to move with the suspension.

The teeth on the three gears used to step down power from the clutch to the under-slung gearbox used a 40-degree helical angle for quiet running and shared the gearbox's SAE75 oil. However, the differential's crown and pinion gear was found to need SAE90-grade oil, so it was provided with its own sealed compartment to contain the oil.

The 1300's clutch was a dry single-plate diaphragm type, originally made by Borg and Beck, and was hydraulically operated. It was bolted to the flywheel and had a detachable cover. The clutch's splined plate drove a quill shaft that was positioned in the top of the transmission casing, and drove the top gear of the three-gear step-down unit, which transmitted the drive down to the gearbox housed under the engine. The use of a quill to drive the step-down unit meant that the clutch could be changed in situ relatively simply, by removing the clutch cover and withdrawing the drive quill from the clutch centre through a hatch in the car's bulkhead. The removal of the drive quill enabled the diaphragm spring assembly to be unbolted from the flywheel and the clutch plate to be removed and replaced.

The transmission step-down unit, gearbox and final-drive differential were housed in a single casting, which was bolted below the engine's crankcase, where the sump would be positioned in a conventional rear-drive engine. This was cast in iron rather than lightweight aluminium for a number of reasons. First, cast iron was better than aluminium for noise suppression, and, as the clutch and step-down gears were close to the passenger cabin's front scuttle, reducing noise was important in order to preserve the upmarket ambience of the cabin. Second, as cast iron expands less than aluminium, it was easier to design an iron casting that would maintain clearances within the gearbox. This would increase reliability and, again, decrease noise and vibration. Third, casting the housing in one piece made for a more rigid structure, with less chance of oil leaks. Finally, bolting the casting to the bottom of the crankcase helped to absorb engine and road noise and made the engine smoother by stiffening the crankcase and giving the engine's out-of-balance forces more inertia to work against. The engine's sump was formed in the top of the transmission casting.

The quill shaft from the clutch also acted as a torsion spring and the rest of the gearbox and differential drive were designed to have no further torsional flexibility. This helped to give the whole drive train enhanced refinement. Along with carefully calibrated 'rotoflex' joints on the final-drive shaft, this also reduced 'wind-up' when torque was reversed at low speeds. The drive shafts from the centrally mounted differential were of equal length and had conventional mechanical constant velocity (CV) joints at the hub, and rotoflex joints at the differential end. Rotoflex joints – two 'spiders' bonded together with rubber – were designed as a substitute for conventional mechanical CV joints. One spider was bolted to the differential output shaft, the other to the drive shaft. The rubber between the two allowed the drive shaft to move relative to the differential output, and also gave a cushioning effect to the drive line. A rotoflex was cheap in comparison to a CV joint, but it did have disadvantages. The rubber used had to be carefully matched to the car to avoid excessive 'wind-up' when power was reversed and the units had a shorter life than CV joints as the rubber deteriorated, especially if contaminated by oil from engine leaks. Despite these issues, the use of the rotoflex was a cost-effective solution, and it appeared on a number of other cars, including the Hillman Imp and Lotus Elan. On the 1300 the rotoflexes were reasonably reliable, as long as they were treated as consumable items and were replaced when required. The drive shafts were connected to the wheel hub through the CV joint and the hub was carried in a pair of bearings in a swivelling upright. The drive shafts were angled backwards from the differential to the hub, to increase the amount of steering lock possible.

The 1300's gearbox provided four forward gears and reverse, with synchromesh on all forward gears, carried on a main and a lay shaft. The gear-change mechanism was rod-operated, and the gear lever sprouted from the lower rear of the gearbox housing. Reverse gear was provided by exploiting the step-down gears – the centre

ANATOMY OF A SPORTS SALOON – TECHNICAL DESCRIPTION OF THE DOLOMITE FAMILY • 63

With its engine mounted on a sub-frame and the gearbox and final drive under the engine, the 1300's drive train was neat and compact. Note how the front spring and damper units had to be mounted on the top wishbone to give clearance for the driveshaft.

idler gear shaft, which revolved in the reverse direction to the crank and gearbox, had a pinion mounted on its tail; when reverse was engaged, this pinion drove the gearbox's second gear, providing a reverse drive. The gearbox was designed from the outset to potentially have a four-wheel-drive function, by taking a second drive off the back of the box using the main shaft. While the abortive Triumph 'Pony' used this design and a single Triumph 1300 was also fitted with the system, the only commercial use of the transmission in four-wheel-drive configuration was by the Israeli company Autocars, which used it in its Dragoon utility vehicle.

The unique design of the 1300's front-wheel-drive gearbox meant that there was no proprietary automatic gearbox available that could be easily incorporated, so the front-wheel-drive Triumphs never had the option of an automatic gearbox. The first of the Dolomite family to be offered with an automatic gearbox was the 1850 Dolomite, which on its introduction in 1972 had the Borg Warner BW65 box as an option – in fact, it was virtually the only option the factory offered on the comprehensively equipped car. The factory was surprised by the number of owners opting for an automatic gearbox on what had been seen as a sporting car, but it actually showed that owners saw the car as either a sporting saloon or a comfortable, well-equipped small luxury vehicle. The next model to get the option of an auto box, again the BW65, was the rear-wheel-drive 1500 TC when it was introduced for the 1974 season.

The first of the rear-wheel-drive saloons, the Toledo, had a gearbox derived from that used in the Vitesse and GT6. This four-speed unit had synchromesh on all four forward gears and was a conventional unit. It could trace its origins back through the Herald to the Standard Ten, and would be used, with various ratios, in all of the rear-wheel-drive Dolomite family cars.

The Dolomite 1850 adopted the close-ratio four-speed gearbox from the non-overdrive-equipped GT6. To complement this gearbox, and to compensate for the Dolomite's increased weight over the GT6, the Dolomite's differential final-drive ratio was the lower 3.64:1 from the overdrive-equipped GT6. This gave the Dolomite an overall gearing in top gear of 18mph (30km/h) per 1,000rpm. The positioning of the gear lever is a simple indicator to the car's type of drive; in front-wheel-drive examples the lever sprouts from the bulkhead, while on rear-wheel-drive cars it emerges vertically from the transmission tunnel.

FOUR-WHEEL DRIVE: THE TRIUMPH PONY AND AUTOCARS DRAGOON

The design of the 1300's front-wheel-drive transmission lent itself to provide four-wheel drive relatively simply, as it was quite easy to take a second drive from the rear of the gearbox, by extending the gearbox main shaft. Triumph did experiment with this, but the front-wheel-drive system they eventually produced was different from the 1300's integrated system, with a separate gearbox that was bolted to the rear-wheel-drive 1300 and 1500 engines. This gearbox was used in the rally-specification four-wheel-drive 1300 in the late 1960s, and the system was also used in the Triumph Pony, a small utility vehicle with a simple ladder chassis and basic bodywork.

The Pony design was a speculative one for the UK military in the early 1960s. It was never put into production in the UK, although some prototypes were produced in the early 1960 and one was used around the Canley plant up to the late 1970s for internal transport. The vehicle was eventually produced in kit form for assembly in Israel from 1967 by Autocars – the company which built the kit-form 1500cc 1300 saloon and also used the Triumph 'SC' engine and transmissions in a number of its own small cars. Presumably Triumph never put the Pony into production as it would have been a competitor for the Land Rover, and Triumph had bought Rover in 1966.

As the Autocars Dragoon, the front-wheel-drive utility vehicle was used in a variety of roles, both commercial and military. It was a simple vehicle with a basic steel ladder chassis with four cross members, a 'forward control' cab made from glass-fibre reinforced plastic, which seated two or three people, and a flat load bay behind the cab.

Measuring about 12.3ft (3.77m) in length and 5.2ft (1.6m) in width, with a wheelbase of 6.6ft (2.01m) and a gross vehicle weight of 4,332lb (1,965kg), the Dragoon was a handy size but still big enough to be

The Autocars Dragoon was produced in Israel. It was a lightweight four-wheel-drive vehicle, using the Triumph 1300 engine and front-wheel-drive gearbox, with a power take-off to drive the rear wheels.

The Dragoon was offered in a number of models, including a tanker.

useful. Powered by the Triumph 1493cc version of Triumph's SC engine, it was fitted with a part-time four-wheel-drive system, which drove the front wheels directly and the rears through a transfer box that could be disengaged for road use. The Dragoon did not use the 1300's advanced independent front suspension but was equipped with live axles front and rear, which were suspended from semi-elliptical leaf springs and telescopic dampers.

The Dragoon was fairly basic, but it performed well as a simple, rugged 'go-anywhere' utility vehicle. Most were produced as pick-ups, with a flat rear bed and canvas tilt cover, but some were produced as tankers for bulk liquid delivery, with a 220-gallon (1000-litre) tank mounted on the chassis behind the cab. Israel exported the car with some success to Greece and Switzerland; some reports also state that the car was assembled in Iran.

RUNNING GEAR – SUSPENSION AND BRAKES

The 1300's front suspension was designed for use with the 1300's front-wheel drive and as such had to cater for the presence of a drive shaft as well as steering the wheels. The front suspension assembly was mounted through rubber bushes on to a fabricated steel mounting bracket, on which was bolted the body shell. Shims were used between the mounting bracket and the shell to ensure that the suspension was properly aligned. The suspension comprised a single lower transverse link and trailing radius arm and an upper wishbone, with a coil over damper unit mounted on the top wishbone with its top located in a turret in the inner wing to give a clear run for the drive shaft. The lower link, often described as a wishbone, comprised a forged-steel lower wishbone arm, which was rubber-mounted to the mounting bracket so it protruded outwards at about 90 degrees to the body centre line, and a pressed-steel 'U'-section horizontal trailing strut bolted close to its end. The strut protruded forwards, and was bolted to the body shell on rubber mounts to provide fore and aft location.

At the end of the transverse link was a taper joint to accept a lower swivel joint. The upper wishbone comprised a pair of 'U'-section arms, again mounted on rubber bushes to the mounting bracket. The ends were bolted to an upper swivel joint and a pair of brackets to carry the bottom of the damper unit. The damper unit had a concentric spring bolted into the top of a tunnel in the inner wing, while the bottom of the spring was mounted on the damper, and its top located in the turret on a rubber pad and a plate assembly, which was bolted in place at the top of the turret. The suspension upright was suspended between the two wishbone assemblies, and comprised a top swivel joint attached by a taper to the vertical link. The vertical link had lugs on which to bolt the brake calliper and the disc dust guard, and carried a pair of combined drive shaft and wheel bearings in a circular housing in its middle. At its bottom was bolted a steering arm, which faced backwards to pick up the steering rack, which was mounted behind the suspension and underneath the engine and transmission. The steering arm carried a swivel joint that was bolted to the lower transverse link.

The drive shaft had a CV joint at the vertical link end and a rotoflex coupling at the differential end; this combination allowed for both steering and suspension movement. The wheel hub was splined on to the drive shaft on the outside of the vertical link and had mountings for the disc brake on its face and carried the front wheel on four studs. This

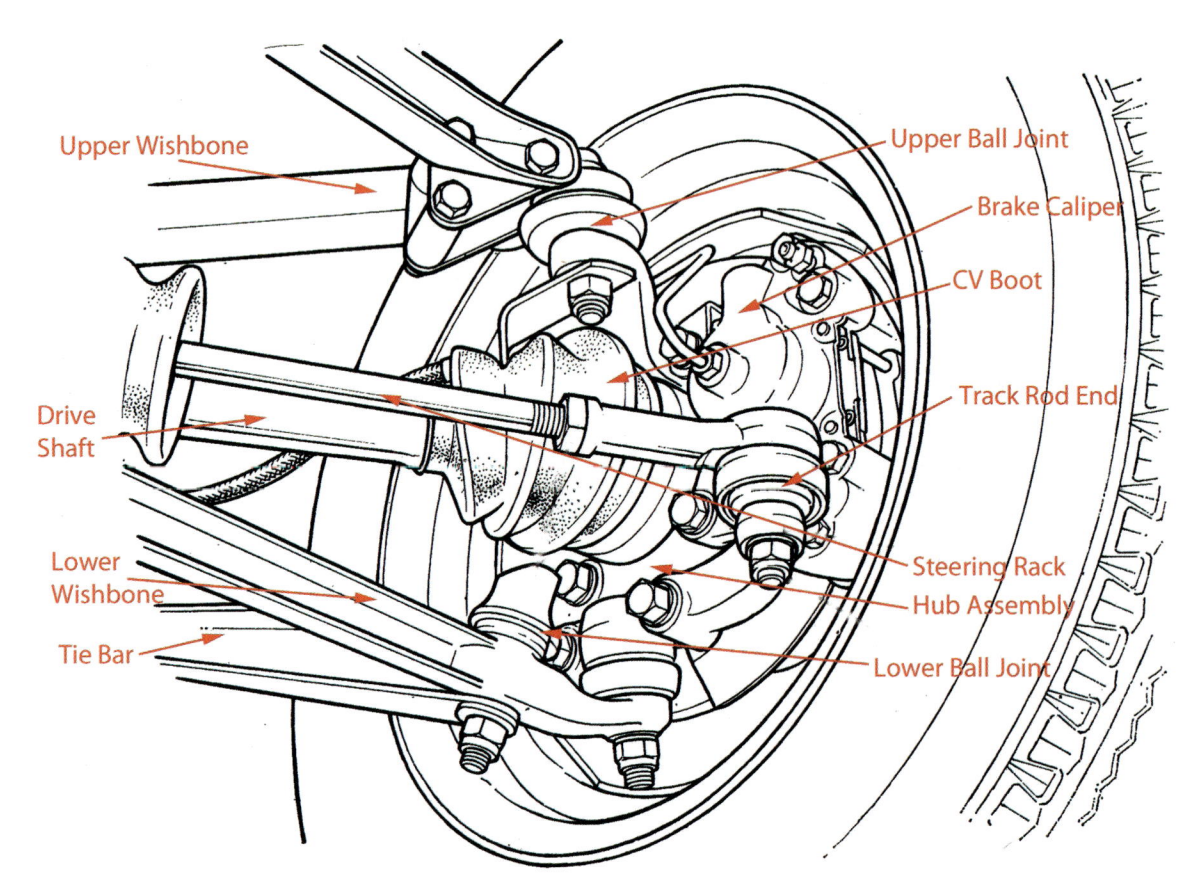

The 1300's front suspension was state of the art for the day. CV joints allow for steering and suspension movement at the hub.

front suspension design was carried over to the front-wheel-drive cars, although the design of the vertical link was changed, as it no longer needed to carry the drive shaft.

The 1300's rear suspension was fully independent and comprised a pair of trailing arms to carry the wheel hubs; it was similar in layout to that of the 2000 saloon. Each wheel was carried on a 'U'-shaped cast-aluminium alloy trailing arm, with the wheel at the base of the 'U' and two circular rubber bushes in an eye at the top of each arm. The bushes were used to mount the trailing arm on to brackets on a 'V'-shaped steel sub-frame, and allowed the arm to move up and down and also located the arm horizontally. The sub-frame mounts consisted of a 'U'-shaped bracket, and individual shims between the bracket and the sub-frame provided fine adjustment for wheel alignment.

Each trailing arm had a conventional damper unit and a separate spring placed concentrically over the damper. The bottom of the damper unit was bolted to the bottom of the arm using a pair of small steel brackets; the top of the damper unit was positioned in a tunnel in the inner wing and held in place by a single nut and rubber bush. The bottom of the spring sat on the top of the trailing arm in a recess concentric to the damper unit, and the top of the spring was located in the tunnel in the wheel arch and positioned concentric to the damper. Rubber pads were used top and bottom to cushion and locate the spring. The outer edge of the arm carried a bolt-on rear stub axle, which carried the wheel hub on two bearings –

The rear-wheel-drive cars kept the same front suspension layout as the 1300, but there were no drive shafts getting in the way.

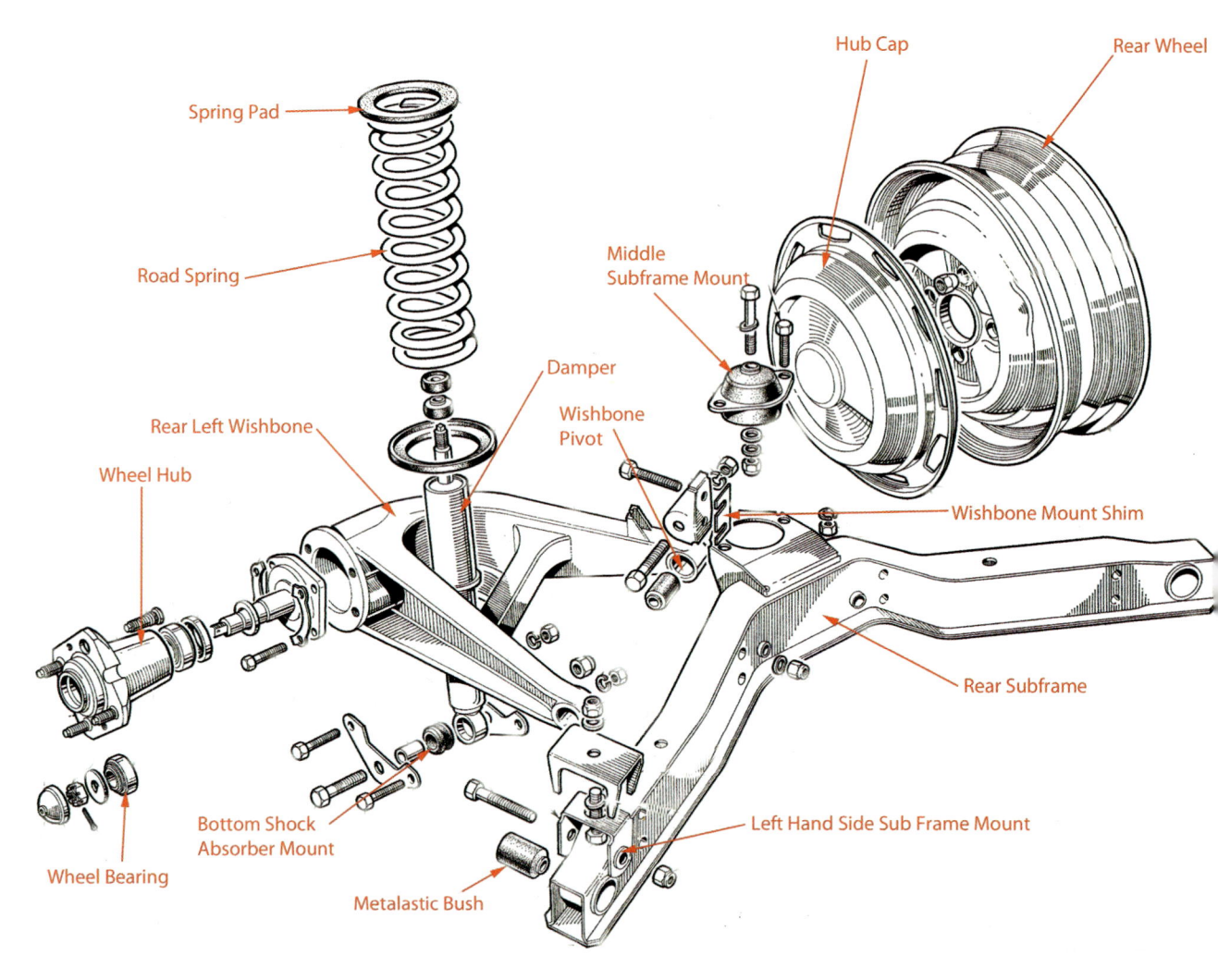

68 ■ ANATOMY OF A SPORTS SALOON – TECHNICAL DESCRIPTION OF THE DOLOMITE FAMILY

At the rear, the 1300's rear suspension was also state of the art for the time. It was fully independent with trailing arms fitted to a separate rubber-mounted sub-frame.

a conventional roller bearing on the inside and a taper roller bearing on the outside. The rear subframe was rubber-mounted to the body at three points: at each end and using circular rubber bushes that were bolted to secondary brackets, which in turn were bolted to the floor pan, and a central circular rubber mount, which again was bolted to the body shell's floor.

The 1300's brakes were hydraulically operated, with discs on the front and drums on the rear. The front discs were 8¾in (22.2cm) in diameter, and had Girling twin opposed piston callipers, while the rear drums were 8in (20.4cm) in diameter with a width of 1¼in (3.175cm). The 1300 TC had a vacuum-operated servo fitted as standard, to cope with the extra performance.

The front-wheel-drive 1500 lost the 1300's fully independent trailing-arm rear suspension, which was replaced by a cheaper dead-beam axle. This was done to cut manufacturing costs as the new system shared its mounting points with the Toledo's, and because the more sophisticated and expensive 1300's rear suspension did not confer any significant advantages to the 1500. In addition, experience with the 1300's rear suspension showed that it was possible to provoke unwanted

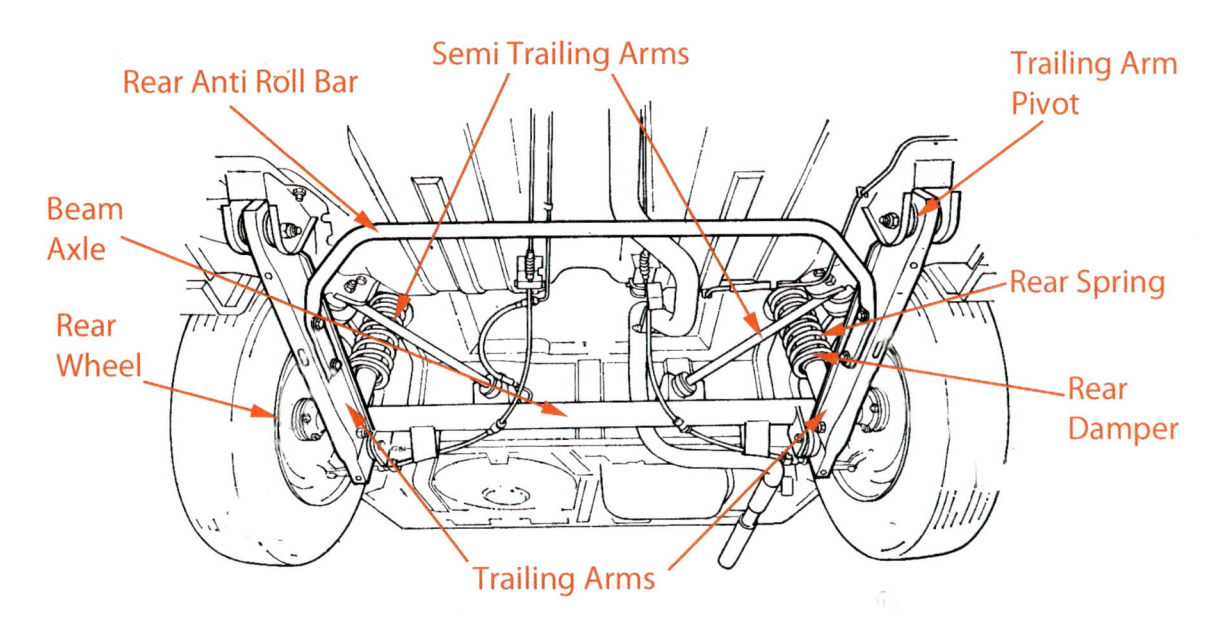

ANATOMY OF A SPORTS SALOON – TECHNICAL DESCRIPTION OF THE DOLOMITE FAMILY

With the introduction of the 1500, a simpler and cheaper dead-beam axle rear suspension was introduced. The beam axle was located directly to the body using a pair of trailing arms and a second pair of semi-trailing arms.

handling reactions if the driver lifted off during enthusiastic cornering. This could cause the inside rear wheel to lift and the front wheels to tuck in, leading to over-steer, or the rear end losing grip and sliding. The new beam axle had a much higher roll centre than the original suspension so had to be severely provoked to lift an inside wheel on a corner. This modification also eliminated the camber changes that the original design allowed. The new system had its four control arms mounted directly on to the body shell with rubber bushes, eliminating the need for the 1300's separate rear sub-frame.

The live rear axle used on the Toledo, 1500 TC and the Dolomites was, like the 1500 dead-beam axle, located by two trailing and two semi-trailing arms. The outer two links, which provided fore and aft location, were steel 'top-hat' section channels and were fitted to the ends of the axle. A coil over damper unit was fitted to each arm close to the axle, located in the rear wheel arch. The inner semi-trailing arms provided lateral location of the axle; they were mounted on each side of the axle close to the differential housing and ran at about 45 degrees forwards to location points on the body. All the axle location points were rubber-bushed and noise-insulating washers were used on the spring seats and the links. The Dolomite 1850 and the Sprint were both equipped with a rear anti-roll bar.

While the 1500 and 1500 TC shared the same braking system as the 1300 TC, with 8¾in (22.2cm) front discs and 8in (20.4cm) rear drums and a servo, the Toledo was fitted with drum brakes all round; it was, in fact, the only member of the Dolomite family to be equipped in this way. While it shared the 8in (20.32cm) diameter rear drums with the rest of the range, the Toledo's front brakes were twin leading shoe drums, 9in (22.9cm) in diameter and 1¾in (4.45cm) in width.

Contemporary road tests seemed quite happy with this retrograde step, but for the 1973 model year the Toledo gained the 8¾in (22.25cm) diameter disc brakes as used on the other cars in the range. While the Dolomite had the same braking system as the 1500 TC, with 8¾in (22.25cm) front discs, and 8in (20.5cm) rear drums, the Sprint's brakes were upgraded. While it retained the same

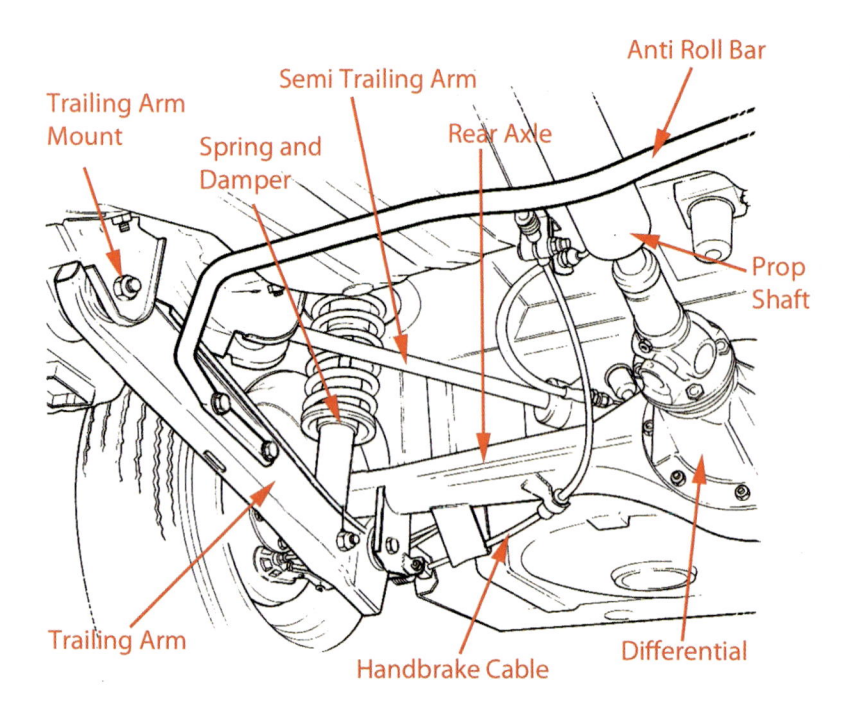

The rear-wheel-drive car's rear suspension was identical in layout to the dead-beam axle 1500, with the live axle located by trailing arms.

Labels: Trailing Arm Mount, Semi Trailing Arm, Spring and Damper, Rear Axle, Anti Roll Bar, Prop Shaft, Trailing Arm, Handbrake Cable, Differential

size of front disc, the pad material was harder, to give better braking and fade performance from high speed. Complementing the harder pads at the front were new 9in (22.8cm) diameter rear drums and, in order to retain the balance of the front to rear braking, there was a load-sensitive brake-pressure-reducing valve.

ELECTRICAL SYSTEM

Supplied in the main by Lucas, the 1300's electrics comprised a 12-volt negative earth system. The lead acid battery was charged by a dynamo driven from the fan belt and regulated by an electro- mechanical three-bobbin type of control box, which incorporated a cut-out to prevent the battery discharging through the dynamo when the ignition was turned off. The 1300 had only two fuses to protect the system from short circuits, both rated at 35 amps; one protected the horns and courtesy lights, and the other the voltage stabilizer for the fuel and temperature gauge, the wiper and heater motor circuits, the flasher unit and indicators, the night dimming relay and the stop lamps. The side and main lights were unfused. Headlamps were 45/40 watt (in the UK) 7in (17.8cm) diameter sealed-beam units, and the front side lights and indicators were integrated in a neat unit under the headlight, which wrapped around the front corner of the car so that the indicator light was visible from the side of the car. At the rear the brake, tail and indicator lights were integrated in a vertical stack on each side of the boot lid, with a reflector separating the indicators from the combined stop and tail light.

In the 1960s, as vehicle lights got brighter and brake lights and rear indicators became universal, drivers voiced concerns that lights and indicators that were bright enough to be seen in daylight could cause dazzle to following drivers at night. Triumph sought to solve the problem by fitting a night dimming system to the 1300 (and to subsequent models), which switched in resistors to the rear indicator and brake lights to dim them when the lights were on. The system was operated by a relay mounted on the right-hand side of the 1300's boot-lid hinge bracket. The relay was fitted to the range until the last of the Dolomite line.

The infamous night dimming relay was located in the boot of the 1300. Here it is just visible behind the left boot-lid hinge.

BELOW: The 1300's boot lid extended down to bumper level to give easy access. Small light clusters were placed each side, and there was a '1300' badge in the middle of the bumper.

The introduction of the Toledo and 1500, in 1970, brought about some upgrades to the electrical system that would be carried forward through to the end of production. The system continued to be a 12-volt negative earth but the dynamo was replaced with a more powerful Lucas 15ACR 27 amp alternator with solid-state regulation built in. The alternator allowed for more electrical acces-

From the front the 1300 was a neat and tidy design, with a family resemblance to the Mark 1 2000 saloon. Single headlamps were the main difference.

sories and, while the Toledo's electrical equipment was similar to that of the 1300, the 1500 gained two-speed wipers, electric screen washers, reversing lights, and an optional heated rear screen. The 1500 also had twin 5¾in (14.6cm) diameter headlamps on each side and new rear horizontal light clusters, mounted under the new higher boot lid to run across the back of the car, bracketing the number plate.

The new system gained another pair of fuses, bringing the total to four, and was carried forward into the Dolomites, with only minor changes, until production ended.

Up to the introduction of the 1850 Dolomite, in 1972, all the models in the range had a speedometer and a matching combined instrument cluster incorporating the minor gauges. The Dolomite introduced a new dashboard, with matching speedometer and rev counter, and three ancillary instruments: fuel gauge, temperature gauge and voltmeter – all standard Smiths units. The Dolomite and its companion cars gained a new, clearer design of instruments during 1974, with a less fussy design and incorporating green lighting created by the use of green plastic inserts in the instruments.

ABOVE: **The Dolomite and 1500's extended tail gave a larger boot than the 1300. The boot-lid lip was just above the large rear light clusters.**

From the front the Dolomite had twin headlamps and a sporty black 'egg-box' grille.

CHAPTER THREE

THE DOLOMITE'S ANCESTORS – MODEL BY MODEL

INTRODUCTION

The Triumph medium family saloon car family can be fairly neatly divided between the pre-Dolomite cars and the post-Dolomite cars. This chapter looks at the members of the family that did not carry the Dolomite name, but formed the basis of the family and set the scene for Triumph to conquer the medium-sized sports-saloon market in the UK. The slogan in each section heading is taken from contemporary Triumph brochures, to give a feeling of how Triumph marketed the model.

TRIUMPH 1300: 'BRITAIN'S BEST EQUIPPED CAR NEXT TO THE BIG ONES'

The 1300 was introduced to the market at the Earls Court Motor Show in October 1965. It was a well-specified and comfortable four-door saloon, with seating for four (or, at a pinch, five with three in the back seat). With the original short-boot body shell, and placed between the Herald and the 2000, the 1300 was only ever produced in four-door form, although two-door and estate versions were mocked up during development. With the trusty 1300cc engine, equipped with a single Stromberg carburettor, producing a healthy 61bhp at 5,000rpm and 73lb ft of torque at 3,000rpm, and a kerb weight of 2,016lb (914kg) the car had a claimed maximum speed of 85mph (137km/h) and a 0–60mph time of 18.5 seconds – hardly earth-shattering but perfectly acceptable at the time.

The front-wheel-drive 1300's turning circle was, on launch, given as 29ft (8.8m), close to but not quite as good as the Herald's 25ft (7.9m). However, once the car was in production, Triumph found that the tight turning circle caused the rubber gaiters on the front drive-shaft CV joints to split. The steering was modified to reduce the lock, leading to a turning circle of 33ft (10m); the car had lost the advantages of a very tight turning circle, but was still good in its class. Fully independent front and rear suspension (see Chapter 2) was complemented by steel 13-inch diameter 4J width wheels with stainless-steel trims, which were heavily dished and held on with four nuts. As standard the 1300 was equipped with 5.60x13 cross-ply tyres.

The exterior of the body was nicely styled, without any excessive detailing, although stainless strips were used to emphasize the car's lines. The front and rear both displayed a family resemblance to the 2000, without being outright copies. The four doors were large enough and opened wide enough to allow good access, even for the more mature customer, and the interior was well designed and trimmed in good-quality materials.

There was no exposed metalwork inside the car. The interior was fully carpeted and the seats were covered in expanded PVC with perforated sections on the areas that came into contact with the customer to keep them cool. The dashboard and door cappings were finished in walnut veneer, to add a touch of 'olde worlde' class. All the windows, including the windscreen, were produced using Triplex safety glass, and Triplex also made the optional heated rear screen. Door furniture, the handles

THE DOLOMITE'S ANCESTORS – MODEL BY MODEL 75

The 1300 was a modern and smart car of the 1960s. The brochure picture emphasizes the modernity of the car and its environment.

As a compact four-door saloon the 1300 had attractive and stylish lines.

Access to the 1300's passenger cabin was good; wide-opening doors and a relatively spacious interior meant there was ample room for four or five people.

The 1300's interior was luxurious for the day. Wood cappings on the doors, vinyl-covered seats, neat flush-mounted door furniture and even an ashtray for the rear-seat passengers were not usually standard on its competitors.

The flush-fitting chrome-plated door latch, with its locking tab below it, and the spring-loaded retractable window winder were touted as safety features at the time, pre-dating the legislation that made such items compulsory.

and window winders, were recessed for safety, and the window winders were of a spring-loaded fold-out design; when folded back, the levers lay flush with the door surface, giving a touch of extra space and a smooth door surface for safety.

There was a triangular opening quarter light on each front door for additional draft-free ventilation. Both back doors had child-proof locks fitted, and the UK-market cars were equipped with static seatbelts for the front seats. Reinforced fixings were provided if the customer wanted to fit rear seatbelts.

Driver and passenger comfort was further enhanced by a proper air-blending heating and ventilation system, controlled by a pair of levers on the centre of the dash. There was also a control positioned below the dashboard, between the steering wheel and gear leaver, which when pulled would shut off the valve that allowed hot water into the heater matrix. This was for use in hot weather

THE DOLOMITE'S ANCESTORS – MODEL BY MODEL   77

From the rear the neat and compact lines of the 1300, designed by Michelotti can be appreciated.

only, according to the handbook. The front seats had fore and aft adjustment, and the driver's seat also had rake and height adjustment, which gave it a claimed 81 different driving positions. The steering wheel was adjustable axially (in and out) by 4in (10cm) and vertically by 2in (5cm), and was loosened off and fixed in the chosen position using a large hand-operated round knob on the right-hand side of the column.

Fold-down sun visors were sited on the top windscreen rail. The one on the passenger's side had a built-in vanity mirror, which, according to the brochure, could also be used to keep an eye on the children in the back. Three ashtrays were

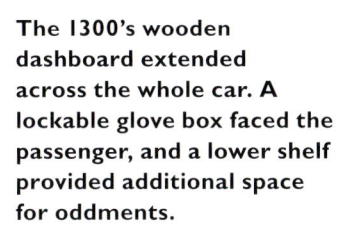

The 1300's wooden dashboard extended across the whole car. A lockable glove box faced the passenger, and a lower shelf provided additional space for oddments.

provided – one on each end of the dash and a third for the rear-seat passengers on the rear of the driver's seat.

The instruments were grouped in front of the driver in a matt black plastic binnacle. They comprised a 4in (10cm) diameter speedometer, with mph and km/h markings and milometer and trip meter to the left, complemented by a second 'three-in-one' cluster in a 4in (10cm) dial with minor gauges spaced around its circumference for engine temperature, battery amps and fuel level to the right. Between the two dials was Harry Webster's circular warning-light cluster, known variously as the 'All Systems Go' or 'Triumph Control Centre' dial.

The 1300 was the first Triumph to use the warning-light cluster, which was fitted to most of the Dolomite, Stag and Mk 2 2000 models, although the 1970 Toledo was not equipped with it. In the 1300 the warning lights were for (from 12 o'clock, clockwise) ignition (charging), low fuel, right-hand indicator, hand brake, choke, left-hand indicator, oil pressure and high beam. In an interview in *Autocar*, covering the launch of the 1300, Webster described gallantly how he had designed the unit because he was 'tired of [his] wife rubbing out the rear brakes through running around with the handbrake on, or scoring the cylinder bores by leaving the choke out'. Such a statement might have proved marriage-limiting today, but Webster did go on to say that the unit was designed so that when a light came on, it would be obvious to any driver that they either had to do something or ask someone what was wrong.

Minor switches were sited on the dashboard in front of the driver; to the left of the speedometer was the pull-out choke and below it the key-operated ignition switch; to the right of the 'three-in-one' cluster was the manual push-in windscreen washer and below it the toggle switch for the single-speed wipers. In the centre of the dash were the two heater slide controls, mounted in their own plastic surround, one for temperature and the other for air direction. On the driver's side of the heater controls was an instrument light rheostat and a toggle switch to turn the lights on or off, and on the passenger side of the heater controls were two more toggle switches, one for the roof-mounted interior light and the other for the single-speed heater fan. A stalk on the left-hand side of the steering column operated the side, dip and main beam functions, while pulling the stalk towards the driver operated the headlamp flasher. A stalk on the right-hand side of the column controlled the direction indicators, and the horn push was a bar with a 'Triumph' logo covering most of the steering wheel's two spokes.

In the front of the 1300 the driver had a neat dashboard binnacle to house the speedometer and ancillary instruments.

Overall, the 1300's dash presented the driver with a modern and ergonomically satisfying driving experience.

BELOW: **Triumph's neat 'All Systems Go' warning light cluster would feature on most models across the Triumph range through the 1970s.**

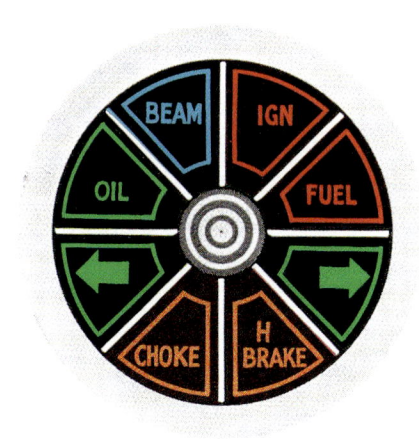

The passenger side of the dashboard had a lockable facia locker with downward-opening lid, and on both the driver's and the passenger's side there was an open parcel shelf under the dashboard. The 11 cubic feet (0.311 cubic metre) boot was a reasonable size and the lid opened down to floor level. The lid was counterbalanced to stay open as required, the interior of the boot was carpeted and there was a boot light that operated when the lid was opened. Under the right-hand side of the boot floor, covered by a lift-up wooden board, was the spare wheel and tools. The fuel tank was on the left-hand side. The rear lights were relatively small one-piece units placed on each side of the lid, and the rear bumper was a full-width wrap-round design, with two over-riders with rubber faces and a neat square '1300' badge in its centre.

The rear of the car, both sides and the top of the boot lid were trimmed with chrome stripes. The chrome trim was continued around the door windows, which carried over the 'C' pillar to the rear window, which was also edged by chrome trim. At the front of the car the two round 7in (17.5cm) headlights sat above a pair of combined side and indicator lights. The front edge of the forward-opening bonnet formed a strong styling line with the body shell, which was angled down and back to give a horizontal 'V' line reminiscent of the Mark 1 2000 saloon's nose. A chrome grille allowing air to the radiator filled the gap below the bodywork. The front of the bonnet had 'TRIUMPH' spelt out in individual letters and a blue and white Triumph shield badge below. A chrome edge defined the front of a small air scoop in the centre of the bonnet. Stainless-steel hub caps, with Triumph 'World' badges in their centre, and a secondary outer wheel trim finished off the smart but not flashy exterior.

The car enjoyed considerable export success and was also supplied to Israel's Autocars concern for assembly from kits of parts from 1967. Produced in left-hand-drive form, the first cars were basically standard 1300s but were equipped with the 1500 engine. This was so that they did not compete with another Israeli car-assembly operation, Kaiser-Illin Industries, which had been assembling the Japanese-sourced 1300cc rear-engined Hino

Triumph 1300 and 1300 TC (1965–1970) Specification

Layout and chassis Four-door, five-seat saloon car with unit construction steel body/chassis, front-wheel drive

Engine
Type Triumph straight four
Block material Cast iron
Head material Cast iron
Cylinders 4 in line
Cooling Water/anti-freeze mix
Bore and stroke 73.7 x 76mm
Capacity 1296cc
Valves 2 valves per cylinder, operated by pushrods
Compression ratio 8.5:1
Carburettor Single side-draft Stromberg 150 CD (TC Twin SU HS 2)
Max. power (claimed) 61bhp at 5,000rpm (TC: 75bhp at 6,000rpm)
Max. torque 73lb ft at 3,000rpm (TC: 75lb ft at 4,000rpm)
Fuel capacity 11¾ gallons/53.4 litres

Transmission
Gearbox (manual) Triumph four-speed all synchromesh
Clutch Single dry plate
Ratios
  1st 3.40
  2nd 2.16
  3rd 1.45
  4th 1.06
  Reverse 3.36
Final drive 4.1:1

Suspension and steering
Front Independent by twin wishbones. Combined coil spring and telescopic damper operating on upper wishbone
Rear Independent, with semi-trailing arms, co-axial coil springs and telescopic dampers
Steering Rack and pinion
Tyres 5.60x13in cross-plys
Wheels Pressed-steel disc, bolt-on with pressed stainless-steel cover
Rim width 4in

Brakes
Type Front discs and rear drums (TC: servo-assistance)
Size 8¾in diameter front discs 8in diameter by 1¼in width rear drums

Dimensions
Track
  Front: 54in/1,346mm
  Rear: 53.625in/1,337mm
Wheelbase 100in/2,540mm
Overall length 155in/3,937mm
Overall width 61¾in/1,568mm
Overall height 52in/1,372mm
Unladen weight
  Dry: 1,904lb/864kg
  Basic kerb: 2,016lb/914kg

Performance
Top speed 85mph/137km/h (TC 90mph/145km/h)
0–60mph 18.5 sec (TC 16.0 sec)

Terry and Guy Stockley's 1300 is remarkably original – here the boot shows the standard panelling and flooring. Note how the boot lip is at bumper level, unlike the long-boot cars.

Contessa since 1964 – a car that was also styled by Michelotti. The only outside indication of the change in engine capacity on the Triumph '1300' was the use of a 1500 badge on the rear bumper. Kaiser-Illin Industries ceased to assemble the Hino in 1968, when Hino was taken over by Toyota and stopped producing passenger cars. Autocars was then free to introduce a base-model Triumph 1300, with rubber mats instead of carpets, no wood trim on the doors, no over-riders and no rear-seat armrest or heater. Autocars continued to produce the cars until 1973, by which time they had reintroduced some of the deleted items in a 1300 De Luxe model.

With front-wheel drive, independent rear suspension and Michelotti's Italian styling, the Triumph 1300 was given an enthusiastic reception by the contemporary press, and was generally regarded as being advanced and modern. The influential UK-based CAR magazine, with a panel of judges including Stirling Moss, Gerard 'Jabby' Crombac (editor of French magazine Sport Auto), CAR's technical contributor Laurence Pomeroy and John R. Bond, the publisher of Road & Track and Car Life in the USA, voted the 1300 as the winner of its Car of the Year Award for 1965/6. It was up against an eclectic assortment of the year's best cars and innovations, including the Renault 16, Rolls Royce Silver Shadow, the Mini's AP automatic gearbox, the Jensen FF and the Oldsmobile Toronado.

Laurence Pomeroy praised the 1300 as an 'outstanding exercise in technical ingenuity', due to its double-decker engine transmission, and as a 'thoroughly well turned out car with an attractive exterior and very well furnished inside'. In its accompanying road test of the model, CAR stated that it thought it was pretty much impossible to buy another car with an equal blend of luxury, space and performance (regardless of size) in Britain. Long-term tests of the car carried out by Motor magazine revealed few significant faults; the main problem was the loosening of the starter ring causing lots of clanking when starting, and the paintwork being susceptible to chipping.

The 1300's family resemblance to the 2000 was subtle; however, while the relationship to the larger car was there, the 1300 had a distinctive style of its own and deserved its place in the market as a quality, upmarket, refined saloon.

TERRY AND GUY STOCKLEY'S TRIUMPH 1300

Father and son team Terry and Guy Stockley from West Sussex have an immaculate 1968 Triumph 1300 in Royal Blue with a light blue interior. The car came with its original sales invoice, which shows it was originally supplied to a Mrs Maisie Green by Stewart Motors of Seaford, Sussex, not too far from where Terry lives, in Crawley, West Sussex. The car was delivered to Mrs Green on 30 July 1968 for the princely sum of £986 and 12 shillings (60 pence) and had a number of extras fitted by the dealer. These included front seatbelts, fog light, reversing light, wing mirrors and 'GB' letters, which are still fixed to the boot in their original position.

The car and its extensive history file was bought by Guy Stockley in 1990 and it was run as an everyday car while Guy was in the RAF – it had more 'street cred' than the Renault 5 that Terry and his wife Zosia had given him, and it served him well for the four years that he ran it. By the end of 1994 the car was starting to look pretty ropey, partly due to the front panel damage that it had sustained when Guy ran into a police car when it was in daily use. The car was taken off the road in 1994 and garaged, waiting for Terry to start restoring it. The restoration was eventually started in 2003 and, despite the car being undersealed from new and not looking too bad, it was found to have extensive rot in the structure. The body shell needed the most work; photos of the restoration show daylight through the front inner wings, the sills were completely shot, the front wings were scrap and the rear-wheel arches were well and truly perforated.

Terry Stockley managed to find two new wings, one from a trader at an Ardingly autojumble – the trader did not have one at the site but was based in nearby Horsham and was able to supply a genuine Triumph 'new old stock' at a very reasonable price – while the Triumph Dolomite Owners club came up trumps with the other side. The floor was OK, but the inner and outer sills were bad, requiring replacement, and the rear wheel arches needed to be repaired. The nose piece on the front of the sill was tricky – it was not possible to buy the specific panel, so Terry made up a repair panel. He did have some problems making the front wing fit – some 'in-situ' welding was needed to get things right! Terry's trade was as a coppersmith, and he had done a lot of welding in his working life, so the Triumph was not too much of a challenge.

As well as the sill panels, Terry made up repair panels for the inner and outer rear-wheel arches, which were welded into place. All the repairs were painted with weld through zinc primer and, when the new panels and patches were in place, they were painted with Hammerite. Terry would lurk in the local stockist and buy cans as and when needed, so the inside of various box sections of the car are multicoloured! When the bodywork

As bought, Terry and Guy's 1300 was used as a daily driver while Guy was in the RAF. The car served him well for four years, when he took it off the road as rust was starting to take its toll.

THE DOLOMITE'S ANCESTORS – MODEL BY MODEL

ABOVE: Fully restored, Terry and Guy's 1300 has an easier life today.

The extent of the rust on the inner front wings can be clearly seen.

was completed, Terry got his good friend Eric Lane, a wizard with a spray gun, to spray it in a gazebo set up in front of Terry's garage, using the original Triumph Royal Blue cellulose. (Eric is a serial restorer, and is currently helping Terry to restore a bus, along with Spencer Hoodlass.) Eric also assisted Terry with the mechanicals. While the engine and gearbox were fine, the car was treated to new rotoflex couplings on the drive shafts, new suspension bushes front and rear, and new brake lines; indeed, all the brake components, including the master and slave cylinders, were serviced or replaced as necessary.

Four new radial tyres were fitted to refurbished steel wheels, and the original hub caps and other stainless-steel and chrome trim was reused after cleaning up. The interior cleaned up nicely, and the only new interior part needed was the carpets. These were made up by Terry in the correct shade of blue using the worn-out originals as a pattern. He did have to be a bit creative to cover up the base of the gear lever, where he cut too big a hole, but the finished result still looks good.

The car's restoration was finished by July 2013. It was due to be pressed into service as a wedding car for a friend of Guy's; in the end, it was ready to be taxed just the day before, but it went on to perform its duties faultlessly. Minor problems after the restoration included a leaking carburettor; the fault was intermittent – Terry found that he could

continued overleaf

TERRY AND GUY STOCKLEY'S TRIUMPH 1300 *continued*

drive the car 16 miles to Horsham and it would be fine, then he would take it a couple of miles down the road and there would be petrol everywhere. He took the carburettor (the standard and original fitment Stromberg 1.5 CD) apart umpteen times over a fortnight to try to fix the fault. Eventually he found that the original float had a tiny hole in it, resulting in the float bowl overfilling and the excess fuel running out of the carburettor overflow. Sourcing a replacement float was a bit tricky. Eventually Terry approached a local carburettor specialist, who managed to unearth a second-hand float for a left-handed carburettor, and modified it to fit the right-handed carburettor that was fitted.

ABOVE LEFT: **After new wings, lots of repairs and preparation, the 1300 was ready for paint.**

Terry (left) and Guy Stockley with their pride and joy.

One glitch occurred after the restoration when the original starter motor failed. Terry and Eric fitted an MG item – an easy job – but, once fitted, while the engine turned over quickly, it just would not fire up. He and Eric went through everything, checking for sparks and fuel and all seemed fine but the engine just would not catch. Eventually, and only when they were checking the timing with the distributor cap off, they realized that the new starter was turning the wrong way – with its front-mounted ring gear and starter, the 1300 has to have a starter that revolves the opposite way to a 'normal' British car starter. The club supplied the correct unit, which has since performed faultlessly. The car cruises comfortably at 55–60mph (88–96km/h) and the acceleration, braking and handling are all good for a car that is some 40 years old.

Despite the extensive restoration of the body, the car is incredibly original; it still has the original blue vinyl interior, which, apart from a split in the driver's seat base, is in really good condition, as are the woodwork on the doors and dashboard, and the headlining. In the boot the floor is still covered by the car's original blue plastic mat, and the original toolkit and spare nestle next to the fuel tank. The restoration is a credit to the skills of Terry, Eric, Guy and Spencer, and is a superb example of a car with an important role in the history of Triumph cars.

TRIUMPH 1300 TC – 'THE REVOLUTIONARY TRIUMPH 1300'

The only major change to the 1300 through its production life between 1965 and 1970 was the introduction of the mildly souped-up 1300 TC in 1967.

The 1300 engine was mildly tuned with a raised compression ratio (from 8.5:1 to 9.0:1) and was fitted with a pair of SU HS2 CV carburettors on a new inlet manifold and a fabricated steel exhaust manifold to give a healthy 75bhp at 6,000rpm, as opposed to the standard 1300's 61bhp at 5,000rpm. Torque was 75 lb ft at 4,000rpm as opposed to 73lb ft at 3,000rpm.

The 1300TC was virtually identical to the 'standard' 1300, apart from the twin carburettors and a brake servo.

While the new model kept all of the 1300's equipment and gearing, the car's top speed was raised to a claimed 90mph (145km/h) as opposed to 85mph (136.75km/h). To cope with the extra performance, Triumph fitted a brake servo as standard.

TRIUMPH 1500 – 'THE "WHO COULD ASK FOR ANYTHING MORE" CAR'

The 1500 was introduced in the summer of 1970, alongside the Toledo, and was essentially a development of the 1300, with a larger 1500cc engine, front-wheel drive and a new long-boot body shell. The 1500cc engine was the final stretch of the Standard SC unit (see Chapter 2), and with a single SU HS4 carburettor the unit produced a claimed 65bhp at 5,000rpm and 80lb ft of torque at 3,000rpm, giving the car a claimed top speed of 88mph (141.5km/h) and a 0–60 time of 16.5 seconds.

The front suspension was the same as the 1300's, while the rear suspension was changed from the 1300's fully independent set-up to a simpler tubular dead-beam axle located by two trailing arms and two semi-trailing arms. A rear anti-roll bar was an optional extra, and wheels were steel disc type, 13in diameter and 4J wide, and were fitted with 5.60x13in tubeless cross-ply tyres.

The interior was changed and updated from the 1300. While it was still luxurious and relatively well equipped, the main change was to the dash, where the neat instrument binnacle of the 1300 was replaced with a wood-faced dashboard integrated with a plastic padded dash top, similar to those already seen on the Triumph Stag and the Mark 2 2000 saloon. The dash was made up in three parts. In front of the driver were the instruments, which were mounted in a curved veneered board and comprised two 4in (10cm) dials – one the speedometer and the other a three-in-one unit with temperature, fuel and battery gauge displaying volts. In between the two large dials was Triumph's 'All Systems Go' circular eight-light warning cluster, in clear view of the driver, and to the left was the instrument light dimmer. The centre of the dashboard had a plastic binnacle housing the three heater controls, and below this was an adjustable air vent flanked by the choke and cigar lighter; below them was the radio. A parcel shelf ran under the

The 1500 was the first car to use the long-boot body and was introduced with the Toledo to replace the original 1300 in 1970. The twin headlamps, which would also be fitted to the Dolomites, are mounted in a chromed surround.

THE DOLOMITE'S ANCESTORS – MODEL BY MODEL 87

From the rear, the longer boot of the 1500 is apparent, as well as the new, larger rear light clusters.

BELOW RIGHT: **The interior of the 1500 had its instruments mounted in a new, curved wooden dashboard. A '1500' badge was moulded into the steering-wheel boss.**

dash across the width of the car. In front of the passenger there was a lockable glove box under a wood-veneered lid, and at each end of the dash there was an eyeball fresh-air vent. The light switch was a three-position (off, park, main) rotary affair on the right-hand side of the steering column, with the combined ignition and steering lock on the left.

Two column-mounted stalks controlled the lights and wipers, and the steering wheel was a plastic two-spoke affair with a soft crash pad in the middle with '1500' embossed in it. The seats were upholstered in vinyl with the faces having perforations to aid cooling. The door cards were covered in padded vinyl that was colour-matched to the seats and each door card had a hard-wearing carpeted section on the bottom, an ashtray at the front, a recessed chromed door latch, a chromed manual window winder and a padded door pull. All four doors had a wooden capping above the door cards to match the dashboard, the floor was fully

88 ■ THE DOLOMITE'S ANCESTORS – MODEL BY MODEL

The two-door Toledo was a 1300 replacement. A much simpler design, with rear-wheel drive and dead-beam rear suspension, it actually did a good job.

The Toledo was marketed as a family car, despite the two doors. The short rear end retained the 1300-style rear light clusters.

carpeted, and the rear seat had a central fold-down armrest. All in all the 1500 was a luxurious car, with a comfortable interior and reasonable performance and refinement. It was perceived to be a cut above the opposition.

TRIUMPH TOLEDO – 'A QUALITY CAR AT AN EVERYDAY PRICE'

The Toledo was introduced at the same time as the 1500, in the summer of 1970, designed to slot in the range below the 1500. It was to be the Herald replacement that the 1300 never was, although the Herald 13/60 remained in production for another year. The Toledo retained the 1300's short boot and 1300cc engine, but the body was revised to be a two-door, and the floor pan was extensively modified to allow the fitment of a conventionally placed gearbox and rear-wheel drive. Despite the body being a two-door, the wheelbase and the passenger cabin remained the same size as those of the long-boot and the 1300 body shells. Marketing material emphasized the Toledo's low price and good quality, with the strap line 'A quality car for an everyday price'. To get the price down to an acceptable level – the Toledo retailed at £889 in 1970, while the Herald 13/60 saloon was £816 and the Austin/Morris 1300 2-door Super De-luxe was £823 – Triumph scrimped a bit on the mechanical specification, with the change to rear-wheel drive, a live rear axle and no rear anti-roll bar, along with a lightly tuned single carburettor engine and drum brakes all round.

The inside however remained quite upmarket, with wooden dash and good-quality trim; the main differences in comparison with the rest of the range were the absence of the adjustable steering wheel, the signature Triumph 'All Systems Go' grouped warning lights, single-speed wipers, fixed rear windows and manual screen washers. Instrumentation comprised a pair of 4in (10cm) dials set into the walnut-veneered dashboard. The left-hand dial was the speedometer, which was calibrated in mph and km/h with trip and main odometers, and also incorporated warning lights for main beam, ignition and low oil pressure. The second dial incorporated the water temperature gauge, fuel gauge and indicator warning lights. To the right of the speedometer were the light and wiper switches, while to the left of the fuel and temperature gauge was the pull-out choke. Opposite the passenger was a lockable glove box. The seats were only adjustable fore and aft, and pivoted on their forward mounts to give access to the rear seat. While the doors lost the wooden capping, the door cards were covered in vinyl and the seats were covered in plastic, described by Triumph as 'Superior Quality Expanded P.V.C. Leather Cloth'. The interior did have a pair of eyeball fresh-air vents on each end of the dashboard.

The price difference between the Herald and the Toledo was justified by the larger size of the Toledo, which had a wheelbase that was 6in (15cm) longer, was 2in (5cm) higher and wider and was 3in (7.5cm) longer, with significantly more interior space and a larger boot. Although significantly bigger than the Herald, the Toledo had a kerb weight of 1,960lb (889kg), only slightly heavier than the separate chassis Herald 13/60, which weighed in at 1,876lb (851kg).

The 1300cc unit with a single SU HS4 carburettor produced a claimed 58bhp (this was apparently lower than the 1300, but was actually the same as Triumph had changed to using the DIN standard) at 5,000rpm and 70lb ft of torque at 3,000rpm, giving the car a claimed top speed of 85mph (137km/h) and a 0–60 time of 18.5 seconds. Some Toledos, mainly for the export market and all those produced in knock-down form for Israel, were produced with the 1500 engine, and an export-only four-door 1500cc model was introduced in 1971.

The Toledo's four-speed gearbox was connected to the differential using a two-part propeller shaft with a central supporting bearing, to avoid the vibrations that can be caused by a one-piece shaft. This was one of several noise- and vibration-reducing design features, which included retaining the 1300's rubber-mounted front sub-frame to carry the engine and gearbox, and careful body design to eliminate any sympathetic vibrations. The Toledo was the first of the rear-wheel-drive Dolomite family, and it carried over the 1300-style front suspension with its single lower transverse link and trailing radius arm and upper wishbone supporting

Triumph Toledo (1970–1976) Specification

Layout and chassis — Two- and four-door, five-seat saloon car with unit construction steel body/chassis, rear-wheel drive

Engine
Type	Triumph straight four
Block material	Cast iron
Head material	Cast iron
Cylinders	4 in line
Cooling	Water/anti-freeze mix
Bore and stroke	73.7 x 76mm
Capacity	1296cc
Valves	2 valves per cylinder, operated by pushrods
Compression ratio	8.5:1
Carburettor	Single side-draft SU HS4
Max. power (claimed)	58bhp at 5,300rpm
Max. torque	70lb ft at 3,000rpm
Fuel capacity	10½ gallons/48 litres

Transmission
Gearbox (manual)	Triumph four-speed all synchromesh	
Clutch	Single dry plate	
Ratios	1st	3.504
	2nd	2.158
	3rd	1.394
	4th	1.0
	Reverse	3.988
Final drive	4.11:1	

Suspension and steering
Front	Independent by top wishbone and single lower transverse link with trailing radius rod. Combined coil spring and telescopic damper operating on upper wishbone
Rear	Live axle with 4-link location. Trailing links carry co-axial coil springs and telescopic dampers, semi-trailing links locate axle
Steering	Rack and pinion
Tyres	5.20x13in cross-plys
Wheels	Pressed-steel disc, bolt-on with pressed stainless-steel cover
Rim width	4in

Brakes
Type	Front and rear drums
Size	9in diameter by 1¾in wide twin leading shoe front drums
	8in diameter by 1½in width rear drums

Dimensions
Track Front:	53in/1,348mm
Rear:	50in/1,270mm
Wheelbase	96⅝in/2,454mm
Overall length	156⅛in/3,965mm
Overall width	61¾in/1,568mm
Overall height	52in/1,372mm
Unladen weight Dry:	1,850lb/840kg (Four-door 1,906lb/865kg)
Basic kerb:	1,962lb/890kg (Four-door 2,015lb/914kg)

Performance
Top speed	85mph/137km/h
0–60mph	18.5 sec

the hub carrier, and the bottom of the coil over damper unit mounted on the top wishbone with its top located in a turret in the inner wing. Triumph, presumably in the interests of production engineering, did not take the option of increasing the damper's travel by locating it on the lower wishbone, which would have been possible as there was no longer a drive shaft taking up the space. The Toledo's live rear axle was located by two trailing and two semi-trailing arms, and an anti-roll bar was not fitted. Wheels were steel disc type, 13in diameter and 4J wide, and were fitted with 5.20x13 tubeless cross-ply tyres.

Never one to miss a niche, Triumph introduced a four-door version of the Toledo to the UK market in late 1971, which retained the short boot and overall dimensions of the two-door. In addition, as with the original 1300, some export versions of the Toledo were fitted with the 1493cc engine to give a bit of a performance boost. The Toledo was the only member of the Dolomite family to be built in its entirety at the No. 2 factory in Speke until the autumn of 1974 when final assembly was moved to Canley; the two-door version was dropped at that time. The short-boot body was dropped in March 1976 when the Toledo was replaced by the long-tailed Dolomite 1300.

The two-door Toledo range was extended with the introduction of a four-door model in 1971.

Triumph 1500 (1970–1973) Specification

Layout and chassis Four-door, five-seat saloon car with unit construction steel body/chassis and front-wheel drive

Engine
Type	Triumph straight four
Block material	Cast iron
Head material	Cast iron
Cylinders	4 in line
Cooling	Water/anti-freeze mix
Bore and stroke	73.7 x 87.5mm
Capacity	1493cc
Valves	2 valves per cylinder, operated by pushrods
Compression ratio	9.0:1
Carburettor	Single SU HS4
Max. power (claimed)	65bhp at 5,000rpm
Max. torque	80lb ft at 3,000rpm
Fuel capacity	12½ gallons/57 litres

Transmission
Gearbox (manual)	Triumph four-speed all synchromesh
Clutch	Single dry plate
Ratios	1st 3.02
	2nd 1.918
	3rd 1.289
	4th 0.889
	Reverse 3.60
Final drive	4.55:1

Suspension and steering
Front	Independent by twin wishbones. Combined coil spring and telescopic damper operating on upper wishbone
Rear	Dead beam axle, located by two trailing arms and two semi-trailing arms. Co-axial coil spring and telescopic dampers located on trailing arms
Steering	Rack and pinion
Tyres	5.60x13in cross-ply
Wheels	Pressed-steel disc, bolt-on with pressed stainless-steel cover
Rim width	4in

Brakes
Type	Front discs and rear drums (TC: servo assistance)
Size	8¾in diameter front discs 8in diameter by 1½in width rear drums

Dimensions
Track	
Front:	53½in/1,360mm
Rear:	50½in/1,282mm
Wheelbase	96.625in/2,454mm
Overall length	162in/4,110mm
Overall width	61¾in/1,568mm
Overall height	52in/1,372mm
Unladen weight	
Dry:	1,904lb/864kg
Basic kerb:	2,016lb/914kg

Performance
Top speed	88mph/141km/h
0–60mph	16.5 sec

THE DOLOMITE'S ANCESTORS – MODEL BY MODEL   ■ 93

TRIUMPH 1500 TC – 'A TRIUMPH IN EVERY RESPECT'

The 1500 TC (for 'twin carburettor') was introduced in 1973 to supersede the front-wheel-drive 1500. The main change from the front-wheel-drive 1500 was to use rear-wheel drive, as already seen on the Toledo and Dolomite. One reason given for this conversion was so that an auto box could be specified – Triumph had been surprised when some 25 per cent of buyers had asked for the 1850 Dolomite with an auto. The other more likely reason was a combination of economic and production rationalization. The front-wheel-drive engine and transmission unit and the associated body shell, with its lack of transmission tunnel, were by then unique to the 1500, with all the other cars in the Dolomite family being rear-wheel drive. Production would have been expensive and disruptive to the main activity, so it made sense to rationalize the range and bring the final front-wheel-drive car into the rear-drive fold. The 1500 TC was created by using the 1500's interior and exterior trim and

The four-door Toledo had the restyled longer front of the 1500, but had single rectangular headlights.

THE DOLOMITE'S ANCESTORS – MODEL BY MODEL

The 1500 TC was a strange mixture of the 1500 and Toledo. It had the 1500's long-boot four-door body shell, the Toledo's rear-wheel drive and a sportier twin-carburettor 1500cc engine. It is effectively the forerunner of the Dolomites.

the Dolomite's rear-wheel-drive long-boot body shell, to slot in to the range neatly between the Toledo and the Dolomite. Suspension was essentially Dolomite, and wheels were 13in diameter with 155x13 radial tyres.

The 1500cc engine was fitted with a pair of SU HS4 carburettors and produced a claimed 71bhp at 5,500rpm and 82lb ft of torque at 3,000rpm, giving the car a top speed of around 90mph (145km/h) and a 0–60 time of 18 seconds.

CHAPTER FOUR

THE DOLOMITES – MODEL BY MODEL

INTRODUCTION

Following the descriptions of the pre-Dolomite cars, this chapter looks at the actual Dolomites. As before, the slogan in each section's heading is taken from contemporary Triumph brochures, to give a feeling of how Triumph marketed each particular model.

TRIUMPH DOLOMITE – 'A HOT NEW SLANT UNDER THE BONNET'

As the Triumph Toledo and 1500 were launched in 1970, it became apparent to Triumph's planners that there was a significant gap in the range between the 1500, priced at £1,124 with tax, and the 2000, priced at £1,587. It was to fill this gap that the Dolomite was produced, as a sporty (but not too sporty) quality saloon with better performance and equipment than the 1500, but smaller, cheaper and more economical than the 2000. It succeeded admirably in its aims. Its blend of performance, luxury and image, along with a list price (including taxes) of £1,399.37 and Triumph's particular skill in filling niche markets, placed it strategically between the other two models. Things did not quite go according to plan, however. The Dolomite launch date was supposed to be in the third quarter of 1971, but industrial problems meant that it was delayed several times, and did not hit the streets before January 1972. When it did appear, it sported a number of styling cues that would rapidly become associated with the sporting models in the range. These included a black 'egg-crate' front grille, twin headlamps with matt black surrounds, black vinyl trim covering the 'C' pillar with a small round badge in its centre, sporting a 'D' for Dolomite, distinctive four-spoke stainless-steel hub caps with matt black highlights and four dummy nuts and a matt black tail panel.

With 'Dolomite' badges on the front and back, these few minor features had a disproportionately significant effect on the look of the car, giving it a distinctive sporty look that made it stand out from the other cars in the range. Mechanically the Dolomite was front-engined and rear-wheel drive, with a four-door body shell and the long boot – basically an amalgam of the Toledo and 1500 shells. It was the first Triumph model to be powered by Triumph's new modern slant four overhead-camshaft 1854cc engine, which produced 91bhp at 5,200rpm and 105lb ft of torque at 3,500rpm. This gave the car a performance in line with Triumph's aim to produce a sporting but civilized saloon. Equipped with a pair of side-draft Stromberg 150 CDS(E)V carburettors on an alloy manifold, the car had a top speed of 105mph (169km/h) and a 0–60 time of 16.5 seconds – a considerable improvement over the 1500. A four-speed gearbox, with synchromesh on all four forward ratios, was standard, and a Borg Warner BW65 three-speed auto box was an option. The only other option available on launch was Sundym tinted safety glass all round. Initially, Triumph claimed there was not enough room to fit an overdrive, but the Laycock J-type overdrive became an option in 1973. On all of the

The introduction of the Dolomite marked both the first use of the slant four engine by Triumph and Triumph's re-entry to the sports saloon market.

overdrive-equipped Dolomites, the overdrive was operated electrically by the driver's thumb from a neat sliding switch incorporated in the gear-lever knob. This was a convenient and ergonomically sound method of operation and was adopted across the range of Triumph sports cars and saloons. The Strombergs were replaced with SU HS4 carburettors in 1976.

The Dolomite's suspension was essentially the same as the Toledo's, with the front being a lower transverse link and trailing arm and an upper wishbone with the combined spring and damper operating on the top wishbone, while the rear live axle again used the Toledo set-up, with two trailing and two semi-trailing arms and combined coil spring and damper units to keep everything under control. Spring rates were increased to cater for the Dolomite's slightly greater weight and its increased performance. The brakes were well up to the performance, with front disc brakes of 8¾in (22.2cm) diameter with twin-piston Girling callipers, and the rear drums at 8in (20cm) diameter and 1½in (3.8cm) wide but were only single circuit. A vacuum servo was fitted as standard, and the brakes were generally considered to be pretty good. Wheels were 13in diameter steel disc type of 4½J width, and the car was equipped with 155 SR 13 radial tyres as standard.

With satin black rear panels and black vinyl covering the 'C' pillars, the Dolomite was a good-looking car with a distinct sporting personality.

It was the interior that really set the Dolomite apart from the opposition and the smaller-engined cars in the range. In front of the driver was a curved wood-veneered dashboard, possibly a bit dated for the time but looking a whole lot better than the plastic binnacles that were then coming into vogue. A full set of Smiths instruments with chrome bezels were positioned in front of the driver, with a 4in (10cm) diameter speedometer and tachometer in the middle flanking a central 'Triumph Control Centre' circular warning light display with a hazard warning lights rocker switch below it. To the right, next to the tachometer, there was a 2in (5cm) diameter fuel gauge and to the left, next to the speedometer, a voltmeter and temperature gauge. All the instruments had matt black bezels. At each end of the dash was an eyeball air vent, and opposite the passenger was a lockable glove box, again in veneered wood. In the centre of the dash were the vertical sliding heater controls, and under the dash above each foot well was a parcel shelf.

Between the heater controls and the locking glove box was a circular analogue clock, which was slightly larger in diameter than the other minor instruments. Below the dashboard was a rudimentary centre console with a rectangular air vent flanked by the choke and cigarette lighter,

From the front the Dolomite's black grille and headlamp surround marked it apart from the slower 1500 TC.

THE DOLOMITES – MODEL BY MODEL

Inside, the Dolomite kept the curved wooden dash first seen in the 1500, but gave it a much sportier look with matching speedometer and rev counter and various ancillary dials.

While it was sporty the Dolomite was also luxurious. It retained the wood capping to the doors, had high-quality cloth-faced seats and enough room for four adults.

Triumph Dolomite 1850 and Sprint (1972–1980) Specification

Layout and chassis Four-door, five-seat saloon car with unit construction steel body/chassis and rear-wheel drive

Engine
Type Triumph 45-degree slant four
Block material Cast iron
Head material Light alloy
Cylinders 4 in line
Cooling Water/anti-freeze mix
Bore and stroke 87 x 78mm (Sprint: 90.3 x 78mm)
Capacity 1854cc (Sprint: 1998cc)
Valves 2 valves per cylinder, operated by chain-driven overhead cam (Sprint: 4 valves per cylinder operated by duplex chain-driven single overhead cam)
Compression ratio 9.0:1 (Sprint: 9.5:1)
Carburettor Twin Stromberg 150 (from 1973 twin SU) (Sprint: twin SU)
Max. power (claimed) 91bhp at 5,200rpm (Sprint: 127bhp at 5,700rpm)
Max. torque 105 lb ft at 3,500rpm (Sprint: 122 lb ft at 4,500rpm)
Fuel capacity 12½ gallons/57 litres

Transmission
Gearbox (manual) Triumph four-speed all synchromesh
Clutch Single dry plate
Ratios 1st 2.65 (Sprint: 2.99)
        2nd 1.78 (Sprint: 2.10)
        3rd 1.25 (Sprint: 1.39)
Overdrive 3rd 0.966 (Sprint: 1.11)
           4th 1.00   (Sprint: 1.00)
Overdrive 4th 0.797 (Sprint: 0.797)
Reverse 3.60 (Sprint: 3.37)
Final drive 3.63:1 (Sprint: 3.45:1)
Gearbox (automatic) Borg Warner three-speed BW35 with manual override on 1st and 2nd gears
Ratios 1st 2.39
        2nd 1.45
        3rd 1.0:1
        Reverse 2.0:1
Final drive 3.27:1 (Sprint: 3.45:1)

Suspension and steering
Front Independent by twin wishbones. Combined coil spring and telescopic damper operating on upper wishbone
Rear Live beam axle, located by two trailing arms and two semi-trailing arms. Co-axial coil spring and telescopic dampers located on trailing arms
Steering Rack and pinion
Tyres 155 SR 13 radials (Sprint: 175 HR 13 radials)

---

and below that was the radio. Inertia reel seat-belts were standard, and the cabin was carpeted throughout. The front seats were faced in cloth and could be adjusted forwards and backwards, and had an extensive range of adjustments for the rake of the backrest and the seat cushion. The rear seat, again with cloth-covered faces, had a fold-down central armrest.

The boot was carpeted, but somewhat shallow and with a high lip, while the fuel tank and spare wheel were stowed under the boot floor. Each door had its own ashtray, and recessed chrome door handles were an additional safety feature. A heated rear window, reversing lamps and electric window washers were standard and the electrical system was powered by a Lucas 28-amp alternator. The steering wheel was a sporty three-spoke design, with an open slot in each spoke and a large plastic 'safety pad' in the middle with 'DOLOMITE' moulded into it. The steering column was adjustable for both reach and rake, the lights were operated by the standard Triumph rotary switch on the

Wheels	Pressed-steel disc, bolt-on with pressed stainless-steel cover (Sprint: cast-aluminium alloy)
Rim width	5in (Sprint: 6in)

Brakes

Type	Front discs and rear drums with servo-assistance
Size	8¾in diameter front discs (Sprint: 8¾in diameter discs) 8in diameter by 1½in width rear drums (Sprint: 9in diameter drums)

Dimensions

Track	
Front:	53.2in/1,352mm (Sprint 53.4in/1,556mm)
Rear:	49.9in/1,267mm (Sprint 50.8in/1,290mm)
Wheelbase	96.6in/2,454mm
Overall length	162.2in/4,122mm
Overall width	62.5in/1,588mm
Overall height	52in/1,372mm
Unladen weight	
Basic kerb:	2,136lb/969kg (Sprint: 2,295lb/1041kg)

Performance

Top speed	102mph/164km/h (Sprint: 116mph/187km/h)
0–60mph	16.5 sec (Sprint: 9.2 sec)

right-hand side of the column, and the ignition key and steering lock were on the left-hand side. A pair of stalks operated the wipers, indicators, dip and horn.

Mechanically, the Dolomite remained largely unchanged until it went out of production in 1980, but was re-badged as 1850 HL in 1976 with the rest of the range, and was given new badging and several minor updates, including black plastic wheel trims and SU carburettors.

TRIUMPH DOLOMITE SPRINT – 'A NICE, QUIET LUXURIOUS, UTTERLY CIVILIZED CAR... AND LAPS MIRA AT 116 MPH'

The Sprint was the ultimate incarnation of the Dolomite family, and it formed the basis of a number of successful race and rally cars. It was on the cover of one of the brochures that the car was described as 'nice, quiet, luxurious, utterly civilized', and capable of '[lapping] MIRA at 116mph'. MIRA is the Motor Industry Research Association, and the brochure was referring to its UK testing facility in the Midlands. This included a track with banked corners, lapped by the Dolomite at that impressive 116mph (187km/h). The heart of the Sprint was its unique sixteen-valve engine, which, equipped with a pair of side-draft SU HS6 carburettors as standard, gave a claimed 127bhp (DIN) at 5,700rpm and 146½lb ft of torque at 4,500rpm, to provide a significant performance boost over the standard Dolomite. The engine was the first sixteen-valve unit fitted to a mass-production car in the UK. With a claimed top speed of 116mph (187km/h) and a 0–60 time of around 8.7 seconds, the Sprint had a truly impressive performance and was hailed at the time of its introduction as a 'BMW beater'. The Sprint was created by mating the sixteen-valve engine to the body and suspension of the 1850 Dolomite and beefing up the drive train with a stronger gearbox from the 2.5 PI saloon and a TR6-type differential. The front discs were the same size as the standard Dolomite's 8¾in (22.2cm) diameter units, but used with Ferodo 2430 lined pads, while the rear brakes were TR6 drums, which at 9in (22.9cm) in diameter and 1¾in (4.44cm) in width were an inch larger in diameter and ¼in (0.6cm) wider than the standard Dolomite units.

The rear-wheel brakes had a pressure-limiting valve in the circuit to reduce the tendency for them to lock up, and the whole braking system had a 3.02:1 vacuum servo, which was more powerful than the standard Dolomite 2.2:1 unit. Exterior changes were limited to a vinyl roof, a small chin

The Dolomite Sprint was a truly fast sports saloon. It was the first mass-produced car with a 16-valve head and alloy wheels as standard.

spoiler on the front valance and alloy wheels. They were 13in diameter and 5½J width, and were produced in the UK by Kent Alloys Ltd, part of the GKN group of companies. This was the first example of the fitment of alloy wheels as standard on a UK production car and they were equipped with low-profile (for the day) 175/70 SR 13 radial tyres as standard.

Going against the trends of the time, the Sprint, like the other cars in the Dolomite family, did not have a dual-circuit hydraulic system for the brakes. This was because, at the time, the Triumph engi-

Under the bonnet of the Sprint the slant four engine fed by twin SU carburettors takes up little more space than the 8-valve unit.

neering staff claimed that the increased number of parts in such a system would result in reduced reliability; however, the Dolomites all received dual-circuit brakes later on in the production life when legislation dictated.

In the cabin, the Sprint was identical to the 1850 Dolomite, with full instrumentation, nylon-faced seats and wood-trimmed dash and door cappings. Options on the Sprint were Laycock Type J overdrive on the manual cars, and there was also an automatic option, with a Borg Warner BW65 three-speed box specified. The Sprint was originally going to be named the 'Dolomite 135', as it was expected the engine would make 135bhp, but at the time of development Triumph switched to measuring power using the DIN system, which produced outputs approximately 5 per cent lower – if the Sprint's engine was measured using the pre-1970 method the result would have been 135bhp.

The Sprint's smart alloy wheels were a first on a production car. A neat eight-spoke design, they took 175x13 tyres.

The Sprint's interior was virtually identical to the Dolomite's, with its wooden dash fully stocked with instruments and sports steering wheel.

HOWARD ROSE'S 1978 DOLOMITE SPRINT

Howard Rose lives in the east end of London and one of his forms of personal transport is a 1978 Dolomite Sprint, manual and overdrive and painted in a Triumph Blue with black interior. Howard had wanted a Sprint for a long time, even though they were considered to be a bit of an old person's car and were not particularly considered to be real classic cars in the 1980s and 1990s. Then, in the early 2000s the cars seemed to disappear off the road – suddenly they had become rare.

Howard had always liked the styling, the vinyl roof and the bright gaudy 1970s colours. In addition he had had an interest in Michelotti's designs ever since seeing a little rear-engined 1960s Hino Contessa when he was a lad – he did not know what it was until he discovered later that it was a Renault R8/R10-engined Japanese car with a neat styling job by Michelotti. Howard's grandparents had owned an Inca Yellow Dolomite 1500 in the 1980s, which his grandmother had remembered as one of her favourite cars. These factors, combined with the Sprint's 'Q-car' credentials – no one expects a car that looks as if their granny is driving it to have a 0–60 time of less than 10 seconds – inspired Howard to have one. As an additional bonus, the car was slim enough to fit in his allocated parking bay with space to actually get in and out.

Howard bought his Sprint on eBay in 2008 for £1,700, without even seeing it. It looked tired but loved and he had just moved to London and wanted a car that he could leave on the road, without worrying too much about it looking good enough to steal, or about preserving its pristine paintwork. The car had been off the road for ten years, and prior to that it had only done 3,000 miles since 1981 and had had its engine reconditioned in 1990. The car passed its MoT test with just a new front brake calliper, but over the first six months on the road lots of little niggling things needed doing, probably due to the lack of use. These included things like the exhaust exploding and the prop-shaft needing replacing; the new owner also managed to bend the steering rack avoiding an errant car. Subsequently, a driver on the M4 ran into the back of the car and then, while the insurance claim for a rear-end re-spray was going through, another driver ran a red light and took out the side of the car. A second insurance claim was instigated – luckily, the two incidents were treated separately, otherwise the total cost of repairs would have been very close to

Howard's interest in the Michelotti-styled Triumph was actually sparked by a Japanese Hino, which was also styled by Michelotti. There was a definite resemblance between the two.

writing the car off. Howard used the time in the body shop to have the complete car re-sprayed, and it was just finished in time to be exhibited on the Dolomite Club stand at the 2008 Triumph restoration show. He was still putting the car back together the night before the show, and was still fixing things like the door trims during the show!

Just three weeks later the car started to make a ticking noise, which rapidly developed into an impressive banging noise. The bolts holding the camshaft to its sprocket had become loose. At that time Howard was unsure of rebuilding the Sprint engine himself and, fearing the worst, he had the car trailered up to a club contact to look at the engine. The whole engine was taken out and apart, and miraculously no head or valve damage was found.

The engine's recondition in 1990 had been a good one and the rest of the engine was virtually unworn and just needed careful reassembly. With the head skimmed and the engine reassembled and back in the car, Howard had a beautifully shiny car with perfect mechanicals, set off by tatty wheels, dodgy chrome and a tired interior. A minor restoration resulted in new second-hand bumpers and the correct tinted windscreen, refurbished wheels, a standard twin-pipe exhaust and the fitting of a good second-hand interior – interestingly, the old seats were snapped up on eBay by Clive and Gillian Raven for their 1300 and used on their epic trip to Asia!

While the Sprint was off the road having the engine fixed Howard bought another Dolomite – a 1980 Brooklands Green 1500 HL Auto. Costing

ABOVE: **The alloy wheels, vinyl roof and small 'SPRINT' badge on the 'C' pillar are the only features that distinguish the Sprint from the lesser models in the range.**

Inside, Howard's Sprint is pretty much standard and original, apart from the oil-pressure gauge positioned to the left of the steering column.

continued overleaf

HOWARD ROSE'S 1978 DOLOMITE SPRINT *continued*

just £300, this is probably the most comfortable car he has ever driven in London, due to its relaxed performance, smooth gearbox and squashy seats and suspension. It has even made him consider looking for an automatic Sprint, but he has not succumbed to the urge yet.

Driving in the Sprint around London's revitalized Docklands, looking for a suitably gritty urban landscape to take some pictures of the car – and unfortunately failing, since it was all either coned off or too revitalized – Howard was struck by how well the Sprint could deal with city traffic. Its acceleration was positively vivid and this, combined with the car's slim dimensions and good visibility, meant that any gap in the traffic could be ruthlessly exploited. While the car took a little while to warm up, having not been used for a few weeks, once it had cleared its throat it ran cleanly and quickly through the rev range. The ride over some pretty rough roads was good and it was even better on those new smooth roads that had been put in since the 1980s. The car demonstrated that it was just as practical today as it was in the 1970s, with the added bonus of passers by taking an interest in its styling, and drivers of other classics (and other not-so classics, such as a dustbin lorry) giving it the thumbs up.

ABOVE: **From the front the Sprint has all the Dolomite styling cues. Early Sprints had a 'SPRINT' badge on the car's nose; later ones, like Howard's here, just had a 'Triumph' badge.**

Under the bonnet, Howard's Sprint is tidy, clean and original. Note the 'Leyland'-branded oil-filler cap.

TRIUMPH DOLOMITE 1300, 1500 AND 1500HL – 'THE DOLOMITES – ONE OF EUROPE'S GREAT RANGES'

For the 1976 model year, Triumph rationalized its small saloon range, which by now was all rear-wheel drive, and renamed the 1300 and 1500 SC-engined models as Dolomites. The Toledo was replaced with the Dolomite 1300, while the 1500 was produced in two guises; both mechanically identical, with the 1500cc twin-carburettor engine, but with two levels of interior and exterior trim. The Dolomite 1300 was essentially the Toledo in terms of specification and interior trim and was the 'base' model of the family. Apart from the use of the long-boot body shell and the badges, it was identical to the Toledo. The Dolomite 1500 retained the 1500 TC's interior and exterior trim, including the chrome hub caps shared with the Dolomite 1300. Both the 1300 and 1500 Dolomites had the single oblong headlamps and a slatted radiator grille. The Dolomite 1500 HL had a higher-specification interior and exterior, sharing its interior and exterior trim with the Dolomite 1850. This included the Dolomite's comprehensive instrument panel, the 'egg-box' grille, twin headlamps, vinyl trim on the 'C' posts and black plastic hub caps. The 'HL' ('Hi-Line') designation was introduced at this time, to denote the upper trim range as first seen in the Dolomite 1850; the 1850 Dolomite became the 1850 HL at this time.

In 1976 Triumph rationalized the range, and called all the models 'Dolomites'. All cars were rear-wheel drive and had the long-boot body, and the 1500 TC became the Dolomite 1500 HL with all the Dolomite sports specification.

PAUL WOOD'S DOLOMITE 1500 HL

Paul Wood has owned his 1980 Dolomite 1500 HL since 1989. He bought it because of brand loyalty; he had owned a 1300 Toledo two-door in the mid-1970s, which he thought was a lovely little car. He had really wanted a 1500 or 1850 Dolomite, but had to settle for a 1300 Toledo as that was all he could afford at the time. Before the Toledo he had had a Wolseley 1500, which he found to be another nice car. He bought the Toledo from a Triumph motorcycle dealer in South Croydon and, after driving the Wolseley, he nearly sent himself through the Toledo's windscreen when he tried the brakes – with front discs they were a massive improvement on the Wolseley! He hotted up the Toledo with a pair of Stromberg carburettors, and he did see 98mph (158km/h) on the clock (on a private road, of course) at which speed the car was, to quote him, 'leaping about a bit'.

He replaced the Toledo in the early 1980s with a new Lada, which he replaced in turn after eight years with a Bedford CF Ambulance, which he could use as a minibus for various commitments he had at the time.

Paul saw the 1500 Dolomite in 1989 in an old copy of *Exchange and Mart*, advertised by a dealer in Ilford (South London). When he went to look at it, it was covered in dust and dirt and had been on the forecourt for some time. It had had one lady owner, but the dealer said he could not shift it as it was an automatic. Paul bought the car for a cheap £1,200. The car was all original, painted in Triumph Russet Brown with a beige cloth interior, and had been treated to a Ziebart anti-rust treatment when it was new – as evidenced by the tell-tale rubber grommets on the sills and door shuts. As an HL model it came with all the extras: a comprehensive set of instruments in the walnut-faced dashboard, walnut-veneer door capping, rear centre armrest, adjustable steering column, centre console, black vinyl-covered rear quarter panels and black plastic wheel trims.

In the 25 years he has owned the car as his 'daily driver', Paul has had very few issues. It now has some 93,000 miles (155,000km) on the clock, and the only major mechanical issue he has had with it is the differential. The crown wheel and pinion were replaced at around 60,000 miles (100,000km). He is planning to get the car tidied up by having it re-sprayed in the near future.

Paul has run the car on unleaded fuel from 1990, when he bought a 'lead additive' solution – a set of five lead balls placed in the fuel tank. He has not had any issues with valve seat recession; the tappets are all spot on, but then he does not go hammering up and down the motorway at high speeds any more. The only other issue was corrosion of the fuel tank,

Paul Wood poses with his Dolomite 1500 HL.

THE DOLOMITES – MODEL BY MODEL   109

The 1500 HL was in appearance identical to the Dolomite 1850. Powered by the 1500cc twin-carburettor unit, the car was rear-wheel drive.

BELOW RIGHT: **The interior of Paul Wood's 1500 HL shows the Borg Warner automatic gear quadrant.**

caused by a perished rubber seal on the fuel filler neck. This allowed water to get into the floor of the boot, which then corroded the bottom of the tank. He replaced the tank with a good second-hand one. The other issue has been the carburettors overflowing, causing flooding; despite trying Viton-tipped needles, the problem is ongoing!

As with the Toledo, Paul has found his Dolomite to be reliable and easy to work on. It is no trailer queen or concours classic, but as his cherished daily driver it braves the South London traffic well, and still serves him reliably and comfortably.

Under the bonnet, Paul's 1500 HL shows off its twin SU carburettors and the general good access to the engine.

TRIUMPH DOLOMITE 1500 SE – 'A BLACK BEAUTY'

Introduced in May 1979 and produced as a 'run-out' model, the Dolomite 1500 SE was a lightly up-specced Dolomite 1500, with black paintwork and a silver side stripe. As a limited edition, only 2,500 would be produced, to give the final sales a bit of a boost before production ceased in 1980. This was a common trick played by motor manufacturers to boost sales of a model that was close to obsolescence.

The 1500 SE was a run-out model, with some extra goodies to help shift what was a model fast approaching obsolescence.

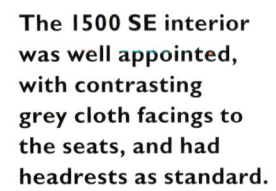

The 1500 SE interior was well appointed, with contrasting grey cloth facings to the seats, and had headrests as standard.

While the 1500 SE shared its mechanical underpinnings with the standard Dolomite 1500, it was given a more luxurious interior, with burr walnut veneer on the dashboard and door cappings, grey velvet seat facings to complement the black seat sides and back, grey velvet headrests and grey, deep-pile carpet. All the windows were tinted and the windscreen was a Triplex 10/20 'Superlaminated', claimed to be the most advanced windscreen in the world. A push-button radio was fitted. The exterior received all black paintwork, with a silver styling strip down each side, which terminated in an 'SE' logo on the car's rear wing. The car had 155 SR 13 tyres on steel wheels, with a chrome rim embellisher and small silver plastic hub covers, taken from the Spitfire. The SE proved to be quite popular and its luxury interior and smart appearance made a fitting end model for the Dolomite range.

DOLOMITE REPLACEMENTS

The Dolomite family was in production from 1966 through to 1980, quite a long period, even by the standards of the time. Leyland were conscious of the age of the vehicle, and the face-lift of the 1300 in 1970 gave the range a more up-to-date look, but retained the existing passenger cell.

The Dolomite design was refreshed once again by Michelotti in the mid-1970s, which produced a somewhat anonymous design with a strong resemblance to the then current Fiat 124 four-door saloons. A single prototype was produced, based on the original long-boot car body, which retained the existing passenger cell and doors but changed the rear and front wings and the nose and tail treatment. However, as it used the existing mechanicals and chassis, it was thought not to be sufficiently advanced, so was not pursued. The prototype still exists and is in the BMIHT collection.

The SD2 (the 'SD' stands for 'Specialist Division', the part of British Leyland in which Jaguar, Rover and Triumph were placed) was a project started in the early 1970s. It followed the successful SD1 design that resulted in the five-door Rover 3500/2600/2300/2000 family, which was in production from 1976 to 1986.

Michelotti's 1970 proposal for a Dolomite restyle resulted in an attractive and modern-looking car.

Based on a Sprint, the Michelotti prototype was produced in the mid-1970s, but the essentially 1960s underpinnings compromised the design, making it look too narrow and tall.

With new doors and thin pillars, the Michelotti prototype was not unattractive.

The SD2 was conceived as a Dolomite range replacement and was styled by the in-house team, headed by David Bache; a Pininfarina-styled proposal was also produced at the start of the project but was rejected. The result was a neat five-door hatchback, with front engine and rear-wheel drive. The car had had SD1-derived suspension, with Macpherson struts at the front and a live rear

The 'SD2' prototype was a proposed medium-sized five-door saloon, designed to slot into the BL range below the Rover SD1.

axle with Watts linkage and two trailing arms. While the car was originally proposed to have a new four-cylinder overhead-cam engine, based on the six-cylinder unit under development for the SD1, in the cold light of day it got the existing engines – the Sprint and standard slant fours and the 1500 TC unit.

A single prototype was produced, and is now in the BMIHT collection. Fitted with a fuel-injected Sprint engine, its styling was slightly ungainly, with

Somewhat dumpy styling and clumsy detailing, along with BL's perilous financial situation, meant the SD2 was not taken forward.

heavy rear quarters, but it probably would have been a useful car in the BL range. However, British Leyland's financial crisis of 1974 and the Ryder Report identified the need for major rationalization of the company's model range and these factors killed the project off. After the SD2 design was dropped, in 1975, it was resurrected in a project called TM1, in September 1975, which proposed to use the SD2 as the basis of a Dolomite/Marina replacement. However, this proved to be merely a paper exercise and no car was built.

By 1980 the Dolomite range was showing its age and sales were dropping, and the rundown and eventual closure of the Canley plant had been started. The company under the leadership of Michael Edwards from 1977 had started to get its act together regarding the product range. With the introduction of the super-mini class Metro, the first fruits of the company's new product strategy had appeared. The next new product was to be the Maestro, which aimed to replace the Allegro in the 'Escort' class for medium family cars. However, the Maestro programme had been delayed and was not due to go into production until 1983, despite being in design since 1977. With the Canley factory due to be closed in 1980, and along with it the demise of the Dolomite range, there was no modern vehicle in the range that could fill the gap in British Leyland's range for the small/medium family car and hold the fort until the Maestro came on stream.

British Leyland under Edwards had already approached Honda with a view to collaborate on designs and production of cars in 1978, and in April 1979 BL announced that they would be building a Honda-designed four-door saloon, based on the new Honda Ballade. It would be badged as a Triumph.

The car that was to become the Triumph Acclaim had a transverse four-cylinder 1335cc overhead-camshaft twelve-valve motor, and could be equipped with a five-speed manual or three-speed automatic gearbox. The car would be produced in the Morris factory at Cowley, and would be 70 per cent British, with BL producing the body shell and trim while the mechanical parts were produced by Honda. While many people viewed the Acclaim as little more than a Japanese 'Trojan Horse', allowing Honda and the Japanese to gain more of a grip on the British car industry, the car was in fact a success. BL had adopted many Honda working practices to get the car into production in time for its market debut in October 1981, and the result was reliable, well put together, well equipped and, despite its 1335cc engine, possessed of more than adequate performance. Arguably it was the

The SD2's interior was fully up to date, with an integrated instrument panel and square, coloured switches.

The Triumph Acclaim was the replacement for the Dolomite range. Basically a re-badged Honda Ballade, the car was produced in Cowley from 1981 and was a successful product for BL.

car that rescued BL at the time – indeed, it was so successful that it remained in production after the introduction of the Maestro in 1983.

Over 130,000 examples of the Triumph Acclaim, the last car to have the Triumph name, were produced by the middle of 1984. It was superseded by the Rover 200 range, which, as an upmarket small saloon, complemented the Maestro just as the Acclaim had done. Built at the BL Longbridge plant, the Rover 200 was again a re-badged next-generation Honda Ballade, and again was produced in the UK with a UK-made body shell and trim but had more local content.

The 1600cc 216 had the Rover S-Series engine while the 213 had the 1335cc Honda engine. The 213 had the same gearbox options as the Acclaim, while the 216 came with either the Honda five-speed gearbox or a ZF four-speed automatic box. The 'top-of-the-range' Rover 200 was the Rover Vitesse, a fuel-injected 1600 version, which resurrected the famous Triumph name for sports saloons and was a small sporting four-door saloon in the tradition of the Dolomite. The Longbridge plant also produced Honda-badged cars for Honda UK. The Rover 213/216 was replaced in 1989 by the Honda Concerto-based Rover 200/400 range.

The successor to the Triumph Acclaim was the Rover 213/216 series. The Rover 216 Vitesse (pictured) could be considered to be the true successor to the Triumph small sports saloons.

JAMES SHEPARD'S DOLOMITE SPRINT PROJECT

After owning and restoring an MG Midget, James Shepard was looking around for another project. He bought his 1980 Dolomite Sprint in January 2007 from eBay for the princely sum of £512.30. The car is a Carmine Red example, with a Chestnut Brown interior, with manual gearbox and overdrive, which rolled off the production line on 24 August 1980 and was first registered on 21 March 1981.

James bought the Sprint because it is comparatively rare, and rather more comfortable and practical than the Midget – an attractive package. The car is a late one – one of the last ten to be built – with a full service history backed up with MoT tests and receipts. Research to date shows it to be the youngest existing Sprint, with the exception of the one in the collection of the British Motor Industry Heritage Trust at Gaydon, Warwickshire. The engine had been rebuilt at 60,000 miles (100,000km), although James believes it is still on the standard bores and crankshaft grind; it certainly ran well when he bought the car, with no knocks or smoke. The body was not bad but was

The shell of James Shepard's 1980 Sprint, ready for the welder and then new paint. He likes a challenge!

THE DOLOMITES – MODEL BY MODEL

showing signs of age, and the interior was also in reasonable condition, although the front seats were quite worn and the wooden door cappings needed refinishing as the lacquer had reacted to sunlight.

Having got the car home, James kicked off a total restoration, which meant stripping the car's interior out to give him full access to the structure in order to start the restoration of the body shell. The car was not too bad, tribute in part to Triumph's pretty rigorous rust-proofing, but it had also been Ziebarted from new, a popular choice for new owners back in the day. Despite this, the body shell still needed welding on the boot floor, rear wheel arches, sills, chassis legs and the front light panels.

Although he has not had it on the road very much, James was impressed by the car when joining

There was typical rust damage to the shell, on the inner front panel and the front of the wing. This was caused by the previous owners not cleaning out muck that gathered in the front wheel arch.

James Shepard's Sprint engine about to be pulled out for a total rebuild.

continued overleaf

JAMES SHEPARD'S DOLOMITE SPRINT PROJECT *continued*

a motorway on the way back from collecting it – the acceleration was well and truly up to modern-day standards and would obviously give a lot of current 'sporting' cars a bit of a shock! James has only had the car up to around 80mph (128km/h) – and still accelerating – and finds it happy to cruise in overdrive top at 75mph (120km/h) all day. The road-holding is a bit skittish; while the handling is overall pretty neutral, the rear end can let go quite quickly in the wet, especially on roundabouts, but it is easily caught if the driver is quick enough. James puts this down to the budget tyres that were fitted when he bought the car, and plans to fit Dunlop SP Sports on it when the restoration is completed. The brakes are adequate – certainly good for a car of thirty-plus years – but probably not up to current standards, so James is looking into any brake upgrades that the Dolomite club recommends.

At the time of writing the restoration was ongoing, with the partial strip-down of the car completed and the overall state of the body shell assessed. So far James has found the sourcing and availability of parts to be pretty good. One of his coups was to find a complete new black interior from someone who had it sitting in his loft for 30 years. The main spares that have been difficult to find have been trim parts, such as the stainless gutter trims and some rubber items such as the rear quarter-light seals; however, by phoning around, he has managed to find everything he needs to date. As James was able to drive the car before its strip-down, and has a comprehensive service history for the car, he knows that the engine, gearbox and suspension have no major issues, but will be refurbishing items such as suspension bushes as a matter of course. While he is planning to keep the car standard, he is tempted to fit a period Webasto-style full-sized fabric sunroof. He is planning to do all the bodywork himself as he found quotes from specialist body shops to be significantly more than he wanted to pay, but will get the car professionally re-sprayed; albeit doing most of the preparation himself. All in all, it is an interesting project, which, with him doing so much of the work, should demonstrate how it is possible to achieve a high standard of restoration with minimal cash outlay.

James and his Dolomite Sprint. The stripped-out shell needs some repairs to fix the rust, but for a 1980 car it is in pretty good shape.

CHAPTER FIVE

THE COMPETITION HISTORY

INTRODUCTION

The first (and probably only) example of a 1300 being used for competition at a national level was when Triumph took a standard 1300 and added a 'Pony' four-wheel-drive system along with a limited slip rear differential from a Triumph 2.5PI, 2000-derived independent rear suspension and a TR5 gearbox. There was no centre differential so the car was useable only on loose surfaces, and the engine was a tuned Spitfire unit, to Le Mans specification, with a pair of 40DOCE Weber twin

A brochure shot of the Leyland ST workshop at Abingdon, showing a Group 1-prepared Sprint.

choke carburettors. The rear doors were welded shut to improve rigidity, and the bonnet sported a huge power bulge to clear the Webers.

The project was kicked off by the Triumph competition department at Canley before the BMC/Leyland merger. The exact reasons behind it are lost in the mists of time, but it seems that it was done simply 'because they could do it', and as an experiment to see if the car could be used in cross-country events such as rallying and rallycross.

The car's first public outing was at the Fighting Vehicles Research and Development Establishment test track in Surrey, where it took part in a television programme that pitched a number of rally cars against tanks and other tracked army vehicles travelling across challenging terrain. By all accounts it acquitted itself well, winning the event. The car was also run competitively at three televised rallycross stages in spring 1969. Driven by Brian Culcheth, it competed at three heats of the London Motor Club's televised rallycross series at the Lydden Hill, Croft and High Eggborough circuits. The car won at Lydden Hill, took second place at Croft despite the gear lever coming off in Culcheth's hand, and was written off at High Eggborough in a spectacular accident when the car rolled after breaking a suspension trailing arm. By then the project had been moved from Canley to the BMC Abingdon competition department as the Triumph competition

DOLOMITE SPRINT HOMOLOGATION

Before it was allowed to be raced in FIA-recognized events, the Sprint had to be homologated. Homologation denoted the exact specification of what was allowed to be done to the car, as defined and certified by the Royal Automobile Club (RAC), which was the UK representative of the Fédération Internationale de l'Automobile (FIA). The Sprint was homologated in accordance with Group 1 of Appendix J of the FIA's International Sporting Code, which related to 'Series Production Touring Cars', of which 5,000 had to have been produced in a year. The full specification of the standard car was defined in the original homologation details, FIA Recognition number 5542, and included heavy-duty suspension with stiffer springs and dampers, which it was claimed were standard in 'certain export territories'. Presumably in the interest of completeness, the specification also included the automatic gearbox as a variant, the 'standard' being the four-speed manual with overdrive.

Added to the initial Group 1 specification, which reflected the UK standard car, were a series of amendments, all of which were claimed to be specified on 'certain export market' cars. These comprised larger wheel studs and nuts, new front suspension tie bars, alternative final-drive ratios, limited slip differential, new crankshaft damper, engine-oil cooler, improved-efficiency radiator, automatic transmission oil cooler and larger carburettors (2in/5cm SU or twin 48mm Weber carburettors) and matching manifold. Finally, the steering rack was changed from the standard 3.8 lock to a higher-geared version with 3.28 turns lock to lock. The specifications of the inlet and exhaust port sizes, the camshaft and the exhaust were also changed to accommodate production variants on 'emissions control' cars. Final amendments for Group 1 were dual-circuit brakes and a roll cage.

The homologation was extended to Group 2 – Special Touring Cars, of which 1,000 had to be produced, and the allowable modifications were the addition of a front strut tower link bar, a sump shield, a heavy-duty rear axle, ventilated front disc brakes, wing extensions, strengthened front suspension brackets, arms and front subframe, strengthened front hubs, wider wheels and tyres and strengthened rear radius arms. All of the modified parts were listed by the Leyland ST organization, and were available to privateers wanting to race the Sprint.

THE COMPETITION HISTORY 121

department was closed, and the project had no further work carried out on it as all resources at Abingdon were concentrated on the preparation of the Triumph 2000 saloons used in the upcoming London to Mexico rally.

The car that really started the Dolomite in the competition arena was the Dolomite Sprint. Its sixteen-valve engine was tuneable, the chassis was pretty good and the emergence of some new race classes meant that Triumph had a car that could, with a bit of effort, be made competitive. The competitions department, still based at Abingdon but renamed 'Leyland Special Tuning (ST)', looked closely at the Sprint and the various racing classes in which it could be used. They chose Group 1 and 2 Rallying, and the new production-car racing series for 2-litre cars.

THE RALLY SPRINTS

The rally Sprints were developed 'in-house' by Leyland ST at Abingdon, starting in 1973 when the Sprint was put into production. Initially there was just one works car used in the 1974 season, registration FRW 812L, which was built up as a Group 2 car and driven by Brian Culcheth. The Group 2 car was easily recognized because of the front and rear wing extensions, which covered large wheels and tyres. A second car, registration RDU 983M, was

Seen at the Goodwood Festival of Speed in 2013, this Group 2 Dolomite Sprint was competing in the Rally stage.

built to Group 1 specification midway through the 1974 season. While the cars competed in important international rallies, including the Portuguese TAP Rally, the Burmah, held in Scotland, the UK's Tour of Britain and the Belgium 24-hour Ypres Westhoek Rally, due to mechanical problems and typical rally damage they did not finish in any of the events.

For 1975 the Sprint gained newly homologated 2in (5cm) SU carburettors and a new camshaft, which gave a significant performance boost at the expense of engine flexibility below 5,000rpm. Despite facing stiff competition from the Ford Escort RS1800 and RS2000, a much more successful season resulted. With a third car, registration SOE 8M, also run by ST, the Dolomites finished their first rally, the Mintex, in seventh place and then Culcheth in RDU 983M went on to come second in the Avon Tour of Britain, behind Tony Pond in a Ford RS2000. The Group 2 Sprint, FRW 812L, came a creditable third in the Lindisfarne Rally, but the peak of the season came with the Lombard RAC Rally. With Culcheth partnered by Johnson Syer, the Dolomite won the 2-litre class and Group 1 outright, coming in sixteenth place overall.

SOE 8M, a former works car, at Goodwood in 2013. The wheel-arch extensions and wide wheels mark it out as being to Group 2 specification.

SDE 8M was fitted with period 'Minilite' alloy wheels, which filled the extended wheel arches nicely.

For 1976, the works efforts were being concentrated on the rally TR7. The TR7 was initially powered by the Sprint engine but by 1977 the Rover V8 engine had usurped the Sprint power unit. The Dolomites had to carry the flag for some of the season as the TRs were still being developed. The Dolomites were used in the first rallies of the season, finishing first in the Group 1 class in the Tour of Dean and winning, with Tony Pond, the Group 1 class in both the Mintex and Granite City rallies.

THE TOURING CAR SPRINTS

While many private teams ran Sprints in the 1970s, it was the Broadspeed team, run by Ralph Broad, that was most closely associated with the factory. Broad had worked with the RAC to advise on a set of regulations for the 1974 Group 1 RAC National Saloon Car Championship, and having met with the factory in November 1973 he was asked to look at the possibility of developing a Group 1 racing Sprint to compete in the 1974 season. His team spent the remainder of 1973 evaluating the standard car to see if it could be made to be competitive, and was formally signed up by the factory in January 1974 to compete in the 1974 season.

Extensive testing arrived at the best spring rates for the suspension (450lb progressive springs with Bilstein gas dampers on the front, and 220lb progressive springs and Koni adjustable dampers on the rear) and roll bars of various diameters to suit the particular circuit. Blueprinting the Sprint's engine raised the power from 124bhp to a claimed 174bhp – staying within the rules, the engine could not be modified but could be put together very carefully to give a significant power boost. Engine modifications were in fact

124 ■ THE COMPETITION HISTORY

Another brochure shot of a Sprint production racer.

limited to a new camshaft made within the FIA tolerances and a modified sump. The new sump was ostensibly modified to provide a pair of oil coolers as 'ears' on each side, but in fact it was designed with an increased capacity to counter oil surge on fast corners – a useful by-product of the oil-cooling additions. Developments during the season included the production of better tyres and brake pads by the manufacturers when the racing exposed failings in the original factory items.

With Andy Rouse and Tony Dron driving, the team won the Manufacturer's Championship for 1974 and in the 1975 season Andy Rouse won the driver's title. Broadspeed continued with the Sprint in 1976, when it competed in the 2-litre class, with Rouse coming second to the Vauxhall Magnum Coupé. The 1978 season saw the homologation of twin-choke Webers and ventilated discs, keeping the Dolomites competitive, winning the first race of the season at Silverstone and taking the 2-litre class again. However, it was getting difficult to develop the car further and its career with Broadspeed ended at the end of the season.

The success of the Broadspeed team meant that many privateers and teams began to use Sprints in the Group 1 Racing class, both in the UK and across Europe. With BL homologating new equipment, such as 'emissions control market' camshafts

The first works team to compete the Sprint in production racing was Broadspeed. They had considerable success in the British production-car race series.

and larger ventilated disc brakes, the car remained competitive through the 1970s and is still a popular classic racer today.

THE SPRINT ENGINE IN FORMULA 3

The Sprint engine was also used with some success in Formula 3 racing, where it was mounted in both Anson and March chassis and tuned by Holbay. As in the use of the Sprint in production racing, this came about as a result of rule changes by the FIA. In 1974 the FIA modified its Formula 3 engine rules to allow the use of four-cylinder engines of up to 2-litre capacity, which were based on a stock production engine block and fitted with restricted air intakes with a maximum diameter of 24mm. It is a set of rules that was broadly similar to those still in force for Formula 3 in 2014. As a 2-litre 16-valve unit, the Sprint engine was reasonably competitive, but was bettered by the Toyota twin-cam engines used by other teams. The first car that used the engine was a March 763, sponsored by Unipart, the BL spares operation – the first time Leyland had sponsored a single-seat racing team. The engine was mated to a five-speed transaxle, and was modified within the rules with a 13:1 compression ratio, polished ports and a bit of gas flowing on the head, a new design of crankshaft and stronger connecting rods and pistons. The car was equipped with a dry-sump oil system and was fuel injected. In this guise the engine made around 160–170bhp.

The March was a monocoque design, with an aluminium tub for the driver. The engine transmission package was load bearing and used to mount the rear suspension, and the bodywork was glass fibre. Formed in 1975, the team used

Alan Howell (Chief Mechanic) and Tony Dron (driver) pose with their Unipart-sponsored Sprint-powered March F3 racer.

Strand Garage Services, based in Brentford, Middlesex, UK, for race preparation. They chose Tony Dron, a well-known journalist and racing driver, to drive the car in its first season, the 1976 BP Super Visco British Formula 3 Championship run in the UK. Tony Dron came equal eighth in the season with nine points in total, gained from a fourth place at Thruxton in Round 4, a pair of fifth places at Thruxton in Round 1 and Round 6 at Silverstone, a pair of sixth places in Round 5 at Brands Hatch and Round 11 at Snetterton, eighth place in Round 8 at Brands Hatch, ninth place at Round 10, Thruxton, and twelfth place at Round 9 at Mallory Park.

For the 1976 season Unipart also provided some sponsorship to the Anson SA1 Formula 3 car team. They used the Sprint engine too, but were only moderately successful.

For the 1977 UK Formula 3 season, with two race series, one sponsored by Vandervell and the other by BP, the Unipart team dropped the sponsorship of Anson to concentrate on the March cars team. The team took on two new drivers, Ian Taylor and Tiff Needell, and used a pair of cars; a new March 773 and last season's March 763. The 763 was assigned to Needell as the junior driver, but was upgraded to 773 specification. The season started well, with Taylor gaining pole position

THE COMPETITION HISTORY ■ 127

The installation of the Sprint engine in the March F3 car.

The two Unipart cars in action – probably from the 1976 series.

on the first two races and second place in the first race, and Tiff Needell getting second place in the second race. At the April Silverstone heat, Taylor gained a first after the actual winner was disqualified for a technical breach. However, the rest of the 1977 season was not particularly good for the team, as the cars were increasingly unreliable and lacking in power in comparison with competitors. One explanation for the lack of reliability was that the standard blocks were flexing as the engine was a stressed part of the chassis, and of course the engine block had never been designed to take that sort of punishment. Despite the premature end of the season, Ian Taylor was ninth overall and Tiff Needell finished equal tenth.

For 1978 the team ran two cars, a pair of March 783s with Brett Riley and Nigel Mansell driving. The team was run by Dave Price Racing and engine development was done by Swindon Racing Engines, but success continued to elude the team. In 1979 the two cars were driven by Nigel Mansell and Brett Riley, finishing fifth and eighth in the F3 championship, with each driver winning one race in the Vandervell British F3 Championship. However, as the 1979 season came to an end, and Leyland's financial woes were getting worse, there was no more money for racing and the Sprint engine's F3 challenge petered out. In 1980 Tony Norton competed in the F3 season in a Dolomite-engined March 773/783, which was believed to be one of the Unipart team cars.

CONCLUSION

The Sprint engine more than proved itself in road racing and rallying during the 1970s, and is still a popular choice for classic rally and racing competitors today. It marked a proud end to Triumph's sporting prowess in the dark days of British Leyland, and gave a welcome boost to British motor sport at a time when home-grown competitors were thin on the ground.

CHAPTER SIX

OWNING AND RUNNING

OWNING A TRIUMPH MEDIUM-RANGE SALOON

The Triumph medium-range saloon family are in the main simple and straightforward cars to own and maintain. As the cars are relatively small, light, comfortable, economical and manoeuvrable, they still make sense on today's roads, and make an excellent classic for someone who wants a degree of practicality and style. While the 1300cc-engined cars are not that fast, they can hold their own in modern traffic, while the Dolomite 1850 and Sprint have the performance to give some moderns a surprise. The 1300 and 1500 engines are simple, robust units and will give many thousands of miles between overhauls, and are relatively simple and cheap to re-shell and re-bore. The slant four engine, in both two- and four-valve forms, is a bit more complicated, and requires some degree of skill to set up and rebuild. The alloy head on the 1850 Dolomite and Sprint is prone to warp if the car overheats and setting up the valve clearances is a time-consuming and precise job. However, it is not beyond the capability of an enthusiast.

The Dolomite makes an attractive and practical classic today.

THE PANTHER RIO – IF YOU THOUGHT THE DOLOMITE WAS LUXURY...

The Panther Rio was a luxury four-door saloon, made by Bob Jankel's Panther Westwinds company, based in Surrey, UK, marketed between 1975 and 1977. In the dire economic climate of the time, sales of all cars, apart from top-of-the-range vehicles, were down. The philosophy behind the Rio was that it would meet a demand for a small luxury car that could replace the more ostentatious vehicle, such as a Rolls-Royce or Bentley, and show the workforce that the owner/manager was cutting back as well.

The Rio was based on the Dolomite, and was supplied with either the 1850cc engine, or, in the Rio Especial model, the Sprint. All the mechanical elements were Triumph, and the basic body was also Dolomite, but all the exterior panels were replaced with aluminium and the whole car was restyled. The nose and tail were completely different, although the car retained the standard Dolomite windows and glass. The front of the car was extended by a couple of inches and an impressive Rolls-Royce-style rectangular stainless-steel grille with vertical slats was topped by a body-coloured Doric-style capping, which was incorporated into the front panel. In this way, it avoided Rolls-Royce's attentions for breach of copyright while at the same time retaining an imposing appearance. A pair of large rectangular headlamps with integral indicators on each side wrapping round the front wing were fitted on each side of the grille to give an impressive and very 1970s-style nose. A pair of pronounced styling creases ran up the bonnet from each side of the grille and this was echoed by another pair of creases running down each side of the car a couple of inches below the window line from front to back. The door handles were placed above the crease line, which resulted in them being angled upwards while on the standard car they were fixed to a vertical face. The rear of the roof line was smoothed off to eliminate the small lip on the top of the rear window, which meant the air extractor

The Panther Rio is a rare car today, and makes an interesting alternative to a standard Dolomite.

vents usually found in the roof above the rear screen had to be repositioned into the boot.

At the back of the car the Dolomite's recessed rear boot panel was replaced with a flat panel and TR6-style rear lights were fitted, which wrapped around the side of each rear quarter. Neat chromed bumpers, which were standard Dolomite items, finished off the front and rear, and a stainless-steel trim strip covered the sills. Three slots were cut in the front of the sill strips, presumably to look like air extractors, and at the rear of each strip was a small enamel Union flag badge. The roof, windscreen pillars and rear 'C' pillars were usually covered in vinyl, and the rest of the body was painted to the customer's choice of colour. The standard Dolomite-based Rio had steel wheels with 155 SR14 tyres, while the Sprint-based Rio Especial had eight-spoke alloy wheels with 165 SR13 tyres.

The changes to the exterior, including the increased length, gave the car a subtly different and quite classy look, and this was carried over to the interior. In true Panther fashion, the Dolomite interior was comprehensively reworked in leather, walnut and high-quality carpet. The standard Dolomite instruments and controls were retained, but the dash sections were veneered in burr walnut, along with the door cappings. The seats were trimmed in top-quality Connolly leather, as were the door cards, the steering column nacelle and the dash padding. The door cards were a new design, incorporating switches for the all-round electric windows and individual ashtrays and lighters in their padded pull handle. An electrically operated sunroof was offered as an extra, and extensive soundproofing was fitted.

The performance of the Rio was similar to but slightly down on that of the Dolomite. Contemporary road tests of the Sprint engine Rio Especial showed a 0–60mph of 9.7 seconds and a top speed of 112mph (181km/h), while the Sprint could do 0–60 in 9.2 seconds and had a top speed

The Rio was an imposing car but small enough to be practical and economical.

continued overleaf

THE PANTHER RIO – IF YOU THOUGHT THE DOLOMITE WAS LUXURY... *continued*

of 116mph (187km/h). The weight of the Rio was 2,855lb (1,295kg) ready for the road, which, when compared with the standard Dolomite's 2,136lb (969kg) and the Sprint's 2,295lb (1,041kg), explains the lower performance – this was the penalty of the Rio's luxury fittings.

With a list price of £9,445 – the contemporary Dolomite Sprint was £3,283 and a Jaguar V12 saloon was around £7,500 – the Rio was doomed from the start and only thirty-eight were produced. The market for small-engined luxury cars back then was the same as it is today: if someone can afford to pay over the odds for a small, fuel-efficient car then they could afford to spend less on a larger car like the Jaguar and use the difference in price to pay for a few years' worth of petrol!

In my experience, and talking to existing owners, any new classic car will need to be assessed by its new owner and it will have a number of minor (and perhaps some major) faults that will need to be fixed. Little or no usage of a car year on year is probably worse than a car that has a couple of thousand varied miles put on it between MoT tests. Often a change of ownership and the unfamiliar driving style of the new owner will reveal faults of which the previous owner was unaware, or just 'drove around' unconsciously. If you are buying a 1300, 1500, Dolomite or Sprint it is well worth finding out what sort of use the previous owner has given it – a car that has done a couple of hundred miles a year going on gentle trips to country pubs and car shows may not be up to hammering down a continental motorway for 500 miles at 80mph without showing some mechanical distress. That sort of extreme change of use will rapidly provoke failures and may well result in major mechanical mayhem!

BUYING A DOLOMITE

The first step to owning and running a car from the Dolomite family is to find one. There are many sources, from classic magazines and contemporary car magazines to internet classified and auction sites. The usual caveats apply, principally *caveat emptor* or 'let the buyer beware'. Before anything, it is important to be aware of a current scam doing the rounds, whereby a legitimate car advert is cloned, offering a car at a low price with a story that the vendor is working abroad or unavailable so that they cannot be present to do the deal. They will ask for money to be wired to them or for payment to be made via Paypal, and will promise to deliver the car – which of course will never turn up. Do not be taken in – always ask to see the car before buying. It is a good tip to use a search engine such as Google, to search online using a chunk of the advert's description. This will sometimes reveal the original cloned advert as well as the new bogus one and will confirm that the second is indeed bogus. If a deal looks too good to be true, it probably is.

Buying from a reputable dealer may cost more up front than buying privately, but the buyer does have some legal protection. Any dealer worth his or her salt will have a reputation to protect so will only stock cars in good condition, and will be honest in describing their condition.

While there are many Dolomite family cars for sale in the UK at any one time they vary in condition and the quality of any work done. First, decide what you want: a project car needing a complete body and mechanical rebuild; a runner that needs tidying and a certain amount of mechanical work; a clean car that is good mechanically, body wise and in terms of the interior; or a concours contender.

There are many online resources about the Dolomite range, and other references include a number of general Triumph books (see Bibliography), classic-car magazine articles and second-hand copies of old magazines (such as *CAR, Autocar* and *Motor*) with contemporary road and long-term tests. Once you have decided what you want, do not buy the first car you see. Take a look at several to work out what represents good value and to see what sort of condition you would be happy with. Joining an owners' club or going along to a club meet is a good way to see a range of cars. Owners are usually only too happy to talk about their cars to a prospective owner and will usually tell the truth, warts and all, about their car.

Once you focus on a particular car, get a test drive and inspect the paperwork. Most important is the registration document (in the UK the V5), but old bills, MoT certificates, receipts for parts and so on, can all give a picture of the car's previous life. If the owner claims to have had restoration work done, he should be able to supply evidence of that work, preferably in the form of before, during and after photos if he has done it himself. Check that the VIN number and engine numbers on the registration document match those on the car and have an independent check made on the car to see if there is any outstanding finance, if it is stolen or if it has had significant accident damage recorded against it.

Checking Over the Car

Take a good close look at the car element by element, and bring along a knowledgeable friend to give you a second opinion. Two heads are better than one when buying a car. Begin by starting the car's engine

The 1300 is a fairly rare, economical and refined classic choice.

while listening carefully: does it start easily, does the starter motor engage quietly or with a clang, does the car settle to an even tick-over? Leave the car ticking over and check the following elements.

Body – Topside
1. Look down each side of the car's body. Is it straight with no apparent bodged repairs? Are the panel gaps around the boot, bonnet and doors straight and even?
2. Is there any rust visible in body seams, wheel arches, 'A' pillars, 'B' pillars, door bottoms, wheel arches, boot-lid edges, around trim fixings and anywhere else?
3. Use a weak magnet (such as a fridge magnet) to see if there is filler present in panels and along seams. If, say, it sticks better to the middle of a wing than it does to a wheel arch then you may just have found some filler.
4. Inspect the sills closely. Give the inner sill where it meets the floor a close look from inside the car, and underneath. If you cannot lift the carpet, then give the inner sill a prod with your finger to see if there is any 'give'.
5. Check under and around the battery tray in the engine bay for corrosion.
6. Check the boot floor under the spare wheel and around the fuel tank.
7. Paintwork: is it shiny, flat, patchy? Is it the correct colour as on the V5 and VIN plate?

Body – Underside
Check all the following areas for rust and damage: the floor pan, as far as possible; the cross members joining the sills to the floor and chassis rails; front-suspension pick-ups on the body; rear-suspension sub-frame and where it mounts to the body on the 1300/1500 and axle link pick-up points on the rear-wheel drive and dead-beam axle cars; rear spring to body mount; front strut top mount.

Wheels and Tyres
1. Assess the tyre condition: a set of tyres all of the same make is a sign of a caring owner; an assortment of different makes of tyre could indicate piecemeal replacement and penny-pinching.
2. Are there any odd or uneven wear patterns on tyres, which could indicate problems with the tracking or suspension alignment?
3. Look at the condition of the wheel trim (if fitted); while they are merely cosmetic, the trims do provide a significant boost to the car's appearance when they are in good condition.
4. Look at the condition of the alloy wheels (if fitted); while the condition is mainly a cosmetic issue, refurbishing alloy wheels can be costly.

Exterior Trim
1. Chrome: cars in the Dolomite family have a lot of chrome (and stainless) trim. Buying new or getting existing parts re-chromed is expensive and time-consuming.
2. Fittings: items such as the bumpers, over-riders, trim strips on the windows, door handle seals and so on, should all be present.
3. Bumpers: are there any dents or scratches, or other damage?
4. Handles and locks: do the locks (not forgetting the boot) work and can they be unlocked from inside the car as well as outside?

Interior Trim
1. Seat condition: are the covers ripped, worn or torn, and are the seat foams in good condition (a good check for foam condition is to check under the seat for light brown dust, which would indicate that the foam is degrading)?
2. Carpets: are they clean and complete or dirty or rotten?
3. Dashboard wood: is it in good condition with no cracks or splits?
4. The padded top pad on the dashboard can crack. Is it undamaged?
5. Interior lights: do they work correctly on the door and the switch?
6. Radio: is it present and working?
7. Door cards: are they in good condition, without having been hacked about to fit speakers?

8. Quarter lights: do both open and close correctly, and what condition are the rubbers in?
9. Headlining: is it tear-free and clean?

Electrics
1. Instruments: are they all operational and working correctly; do the instrument lights work and can they be dimmed using the rheostat?
2. Rear heated screen (if fitted): is it working?
3. Are all lights and indicators working?
4. Warning lights: check that the lights in the round dash cluster are all working. A non-operational oil warning light should be viewed with suspicion.
5. Horn: is it working and loud?
6. Electric fan (if fitted): a good-quality fan (such as a Kenlowe) should have a thermostatic control, which can be manually adjusted.
7. Electronic ignition (if fitted): how old is it and is it properly wired in?
8. General state of wiring: is it neat and tidy or a rat's nest?

Engine
1. Engine bay: is it tidy and looked after or oily and neglected; is everything in place and neatly tied down?
2. Oil pressure: if a gauge is fitted, check the pressure at tick-over (over 10psi) and at high revs (40–55psi). If no gauge is fitted, then turn off the engine, flick the ignition back on and see how long it takes for the oil-pressure light to go on; then restart the engine and check how quickly the oil light goes off. Slow to come on and quick to go off is good. The oil light operates at around 3–5psi so if it flickers or is on at tick-over, the big-end and/or main bearings may be worn.
3. Is the timing chain quiet on the slant four engine? If so, ask when it was last changed.
4. Is the engine oil up to level and clean?
5. Is the engine quiet and smooth-running?
6. Are there any significant oil leaks? If so, why has the owner not fixed them?
7. Is the radiator water clean and does it have anti-freeze in it?

8. There should be no smell of exhaust gases in the water; if there is, it could mean a head gasket is on the way out.

Gearbox
1. Check the auto box fluid level and that the ATF on the dipstick is cherry red not brown.
2. Check the auto box adjustment: do the gears selected correspond to the markings on the selector and does the starter only operate in Park and Neutral?
3. Check that the auto box selects gears smoothly and changes cleanly.
4. Does the auto box kick-down work correctly?
5. Check manual box synchromesh on all four gears during the test run.
6. Check operation of the overdrive during the test drive – it should engage in third and fourth gears only.
7. Listen for whines or other noises on the test drive.

Steering and Suspension
On rear-wheel-drive cars, check the rear differential and prop shaft by listening for whines, clonks and other noises on the test drive. A driveline vibration at certain speeds may be an out of balance prop shaft.

On front-wheel drive cars, check the steering CV joint rubbers for splits. Check the condition of the inboard rubber donuts – they can be expensive to replace if they are showing signs of cracking.

Front suspension: rock the front wheels to test for play in suspension, steering linkages and wheel bearings. Bounce the front wings to check the front strut – the car should settle quickly with no oscillations, and there should be no clunks.

Rear suspension: do the 'bounce' test on each rear wing to check the shock absorbers. While the car is jacked up, spin a rear wheel to check the differential and wheel bearings. Try to move the wheel from side to side to test for any other suspension play.

Brakes
1. Check the state of the brake fluid – is it clean?
2. Test the servo by starting the car up with your foot on the brake pedal; there should be a slight movement of the pedal if the servo is working.
3. Try to look at the front discs (this is easy with the alloys on the Sprint) and check for a wear lip on the outside edge and grooving on the disc surface.
4. Check the front pads to make sure there is plenty of friction material left.
5. Pull on the handbrake; it should only go up a few 'clicks' on the lever before it is on, and the brake should hold the car on an incline.
6. With the handbrake on, look under the back of the car and tug on each handbrake cable to make sure they are both taut.
7. Check the backs of the rear drums for fluid leaks.

Exhaust
1. The exhaust should be quiet and not leaking. Bear in mind that replacing pieces of mild-steel exhaust is a thankless task and it will probably be worth fitting a complete stainless-steel system if part of the exhaust is suspect. An existing stainless-steel exhaust is a good thing.
2. Make sure the exhaust is properly hung and clamped up so that it does not hit anything.

Taking a Test Drive

By the time you have carried out all the checks, the car should be really well warmed up, the electric fan (if fitted) should have cut in and if the car has not boiled over then the cooling system is probably working correctly. It is now time to take it for a test drive. Make sure you are insured – if you are not, then get the owner to drive. In the test drive you are looking to identify creaks, groans and flexing from the body, which could indicate a weakened structure due to rust; any clunks or knocks from the suspension could reflect worn top or bottom swivel joints or ageing rubber bushes; any grumbling wheel bearings and whines from the transmission and final drive may indicate excessive wear. The engine of all types, slant four or the 1300/1500, should pull strongly and not have any misfires, and should rev cleanly up to the red line. The exhaust should be quiet and there should be minimal smoke out of the exhaust.

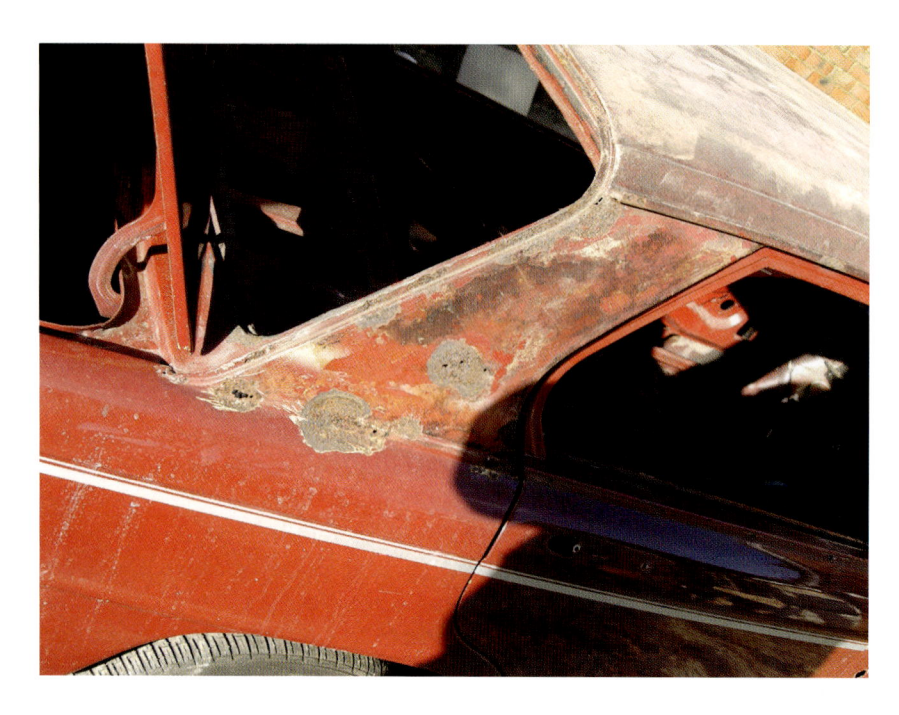

Typical rust issues from water getting under the Dolomite's vinyl 'C' pillar covers.

OWNING AND RUNNING ■ 137

The unassisted steering will probably feel heavy if you are used to power steering, but it should be smooth, not notchy. Any tight spots or vagueness in the straight-ahead position indicates a worn rack. Like the steering, the brakes will seem heavy in comparison to those on a modern car but should pull the car up straight and reasonably quickly. The clutch (if it is a manual) should be reasonably light and the gearbox should have synchromesh on all four forward gears. If fitted, the overdrive should operate on third and top and should flick in and out quickly and cleanly when the switch is used. If the car is an automatic, then gear changes should be reasonably quick and smooth, and the kick-down should operate if the throttle is floored. Each gear should be where the gear lever says it is – poorly adjusted boxes can appear to 'lose' Park. Also the inhibitor switch on the auto cars should prevent the car starting in any gear other than 'P' or 'N', but it is relatively easy to disconnect it so it is worth checking if the car will start in gear.

The good thing is that just about all mechanical and electrical parts are still available and are generally reasonably priced. Virtually any mechanical fault can be fixed either by a mechanically competent owner, or by a local garage, and most repairs (apart from an engine or gearbox rebuild) will be relatively cheap. While Triumph did have better rust-proofing than its competitors, the cars are all over 35 years old, so rust will inevitably be an issue. If there is rust in the car, it will cost a significant amount to get it fixed properly – chasing rust is a thankless task and will most likely result in extensive work, however, it is possible to fix local areas of rust reasonably economically. Trim items are a bit more problematic, especially on the earlier cars. It is expensive to get a trimmer to do any work (such as replacing or repairing seat trims) but it should not be beyond the capabilities of a competent owner. New carpets are a quick, reasonably priced way of giving a tired interior a quick lift and fitting is a straightforward job.

Finally, if all the checks are satisfactory and the test drive is OK, do you like the colour? Yes? Is the price right? Then go ahead and buy it…!

More rust – the rear of the sills can be attacked by the tin worm if the owner fails to clean under the wheel arches.

CLIVE AND GILLIAN RAVEN'S 1300

Clive and Gillian Raven own a 1967 Triumph 1300 in Valencia Blue with the original 1296cc engine. Nothing out of the ordinary there, but it is what they have used it for that marks it and them as something special. In June 2013 they decided to take the newly restored car from their home in Sheffield in the UK to Singapore, running up a total mileage of 17,356 (27,943km). The trip lasted until September, when the 1300 was boxed up and returned to the UK by sea. They didn't take the direct route – travelling for the joy of it resulted in them driving through France, Germany, the Czech Republic, Poland, Lithuania, Latvia, Estonia, Russia, Mongolia, China, Laos, Thailand, Cambodia and Malaysia before getting to Singapore. The car behaved well, with just some running repairs needed to the suspension in the Gobi Desert, fuel starvation in China and a repair to the crankshaft pulley in Laos.

The car was originally bought for £540 on eBay in January 2008, intended as a winter hack that would be more practical than the Herald convertible the Ravens already owned. In the first year of ownership Clive had to weld up the sills and wheel arches, and the gearbox was replaced with a second-hand unit after the original failed on a wet Friday evening on the A38 near Derby, on the way to Cornwall. To give the car its due, that was its only major failure. As the car was starting to look tatty, in late 2012 Clive decided to restore it and then take it on the world trip. He rebuilt the engine with new rings, shells and timing chains and

Clive and Gillian Raven's 1300 made it from the UK to Singapore in 2013. Note the Chinese script on the rear window, written by their guide in China to explain to any onlookers what it was doing there.

had the head converted to unleaded. He replaced the front wings, repaired the rusty doors and fitted a full-size Webasto sunroof that had originally been fitted to a Herald. He also fitted an aftermarket servo and 155/80 x13 radial tyres.

The Ravens find that the car has excellent handling, with good cornering, with only a touch of under-steer and, with the servo, the brakes are fully able to cope with the car's performance. With a top speed of around 85mph (137km/h) and a comfortable cruising speed of 70mph (113km/h), it proved itself to be a great long-distance vehicle. With its comfy cabin (with Howard Rose's Dolomite Sprint front seats), amazing character and quality build, it would be hard to find a better car for such a trip. Probably the best moment in the car was when they had completed the journey across the Gobi Desert in Mongolia, when the car was severely tested by the unmade roads and the heat, but coped with everything thrown at it. One interesting souvenir from the trip was the Chinese script on the windows, which describes what the car was doing. The Ravens were amazed by the interest shown in them and the car while they traversed China; their guide wrote an explanation on the car to save telling the story again and again!

All in all, the Ravens have demonstrated that it is not necessary to have an exotic, fully equipped four-wheel-drive vehicle and a massive back-up team in order to have an adventure. Contrary to expectations, a good simple classic car is ideal for the task and a Triumph is the car of choice of the experts!

Clive and Gillian Raven's 1300's driving position – many miles were covered but the whole car was pretty much standard.

DOLOMITE CLUBS

There are a large number of Triumph car clubs, all of which can have something to offer the Dolomite owner. The main club catering for the Dolomite family is the Triumph Dolomite Club, which offers a bi-monthy magazine, local area groups across the UK, and technical advice as well as discounted insurance schemes, spares locator and re-manufacturing, and a presence at most of the UK's major classic car shows.

Triumph Dolomite Club
Suite 920 Kemp House
152 City Road
London EC1V 2NX
United Kingdom

Telephone: 08700 111737
Fax: 0844 2724930
Membership enquiries: 07769 156505
Website: triumphdolomite.co.uk/dolomite

Other UK-based clubs that also cater for the Dolomite include the Triumph Sports Six Club (TSSC.org.uk) and Club Triumph (triumph.org.uk).

Finally, probably one of the best websites for all things British Leyland is aronline.co.uk, which has many contributors and hosts a vast range of information, anecdotes and pictures of the products of the motor industry.

BIBLIOGRAPHY

The following books provide a great deal of background information on the evolution of the British car industry, Triumph cars in general, the birth and eventual decline of British Leyland, and are all relevant to the design and development of the Dolomite range:

Triumph Cars – The Complete Story (subtitled 'From Tri-car to Acclaim'), Graham Robson and Richard Langworth, Motor Racing Publications Ltd, ISBN 0-947-98128-4. Written by acknowledged Triumph expert Graham Robson, this book charts the entire history of Triumph car production from 1923 to the Honda-based Acclaim of the 1980s.

The Works Triumphs – 50 Years in Motorsport, Graham Robson, Haynes, ISBN 0-854-29926-2. Published in 1993, this book describes Triumph's (and Standard's) motor sport achievements in a readable and easily digested form.

The Book of the Standard Motor Company, Graham Robson, Veloce Publishing, ISBN 978-1-845-84343-4. Published in 2011, this book looks at the products of the Standard motor company from 1903 to the eventual disappearance of the name in 1963.

The Leyland Papers, Graham Turner, Eyre and Spottiswoode, ISBN 0-413-28020-9. Published in 1971, this book looks in detail at the formation of the British Leyland Motor Corporation and is based on a meticulous study of the minutes and papers of Leyland Motor Company and British Motor Holdings as well as early British Leyland minutes and papers from just after the merger.

The Rise and Decline of the British Motor Industry, Roy Church, Cambridge University Press, ISBN 0-521-55770-4 (paperback), 0521-55283-4 (hardback). Published in 1995, this book looks at the social and economic history of the British car industry, with a particular emphasis on the creation of British Leyland.

British Leyland: Chronicle of a Car Crash 1968–1978, Chris Cowin, ISBN 978-1-477-56067-9. Self-published in 2012, this book attempts to chart the facts behind the formation, operation and eventual demise of British Leyland.

Back from the Brink, Michael Edwards, William Collins and Sons, ISBN 0-002-17074-4. Published in 1983, this book was written by the BL chairman appointed by the government in 1977 and describes how he struggled to get British Leyland into a state in which it had some chance of survival. It gives a great insight into how BL as a whole was operating in the years since its formation.

British Leyland – The Truth About the Cars, Jeff Daniels, Osprey Publishing, ISBN 0-850-45392-5. Published in 1980, this book looks at the formation of British Leyland, the cars and the issues behind the cars of the time, in an informed and readable form.

Motor magazine, 15 June 1968. This issue of *Motor* has a supplement looking at Triumph, including an article on Triumph and Michelotti and an interview with Harry Webster and Spen King. It also has a detailed article on the development of the Saab version of the Triumph slant four engine.

Autocar, 18 February 1966. This issue has a comprehensive interview with Harry Webster about the design, engineering and production of the 1300.

Autocar magazine, 6 January 1972. This issue has the launch details of the Triumph Dolomite 1850.

Autocar magazine, 20 August 1970. This issue has the launch details of the 1500 and Toledo.

CAR magazine, March 1966, carried a number of articles on the 1300 and how it won their CAR of the Year Award, along with a road test and interview with Harry Webster.

INDEX

Abingdon 110, 120, 121
Alfa Romeo 27, 45
Alfa Romeo models:
  8C 26
  Alfasud 14
  Giulia 50, 51
Anson 125, 126
Austin, Austin Morris 16, 22, 89
Austin Rover 30
Austin models:
  1100/1300 14, 24
  A30 42
  Allegro 51
  Maestro 30
  Mini 60, 81
  Metro 114
  Seven 7
  Vanden Plas 14
Autocar magazine 24, 35, 49, 63, 78, 133, 141
Autocars 63, 79, 81
Autocars Dragoon 63, 64, 65
Avon Tour of Britain rally 122

Bergerac 18
Bilstein 123
Black, Sir John 17, 18
BMC 14, 20, 32, 42, 60, 120
BMH 8, 141
BMIHT 6, 33, 111, 113
British Leyland 8, 9, 14, 15, 29, 30, 32, 49, 50, 55, 56, 111, 114, 128, 140, 141
Broadspeed 123, 124, 215
Burmah Rally 122

Canley 7, 8, 40, 42, 64, 89, 114, 120
Cowley 8, 30, 114, 115
Croft Circuit 120

Crombac, Gerald (Jabby) 81
Culcheth, Brian 120, 121, 122

Dawtrey, Lewis 44
Design Council Award 58, 59
DIN 43, 60, 89, 101, 103
Dron, Tony 124, 126

Eggborough Circuit 120
Eley, David 43

FIA 120, 124, 125
Four Wheel Drive 63, 64, 65, 110, 139

Gilberg, Andy 6

Hassan, Walter 55, 56
Hillman 14, 27, 62
Holbay 125
Honda 8, 16, 30, 58, 114, 115
Honda models:
  Ballade 30, 114, 115
  Concerto 115

Jankell, Bob 130

Kaiser-Illin Industries 79, 81
King, Spen 45, 55, 56, 141
Koni 123

Land Rover 64
Leyland Motors 21, 32, 106, 111, 110, 120, 121, 125, 128
Lindisfarne Rally 122
London Motor Club 120
Lotus 45, 56
Lotus Elan 35, 56, 62
Lydden 120

Lyons, Sir William 17, 18

Mallory Park Circuit 126
Mansell, Nigel 128
March 6, 125–128
MG 85
MG models:
   Midget 42, 116
   MG 'T' 19
Michelotti, Giovanni 6, 8, 9, 10, 20, 22, 24, 25, 32, 77, 79,
    81, 104, 111, 112, 141
Mintex Rally 122, 123
MIRA. 101
Morris 8, 16, 114
Morris models:
   1100/1300 14, 22, 24, 30, 89
   Marina 278
   Minor 42
Motor magazine 45, 49, 81, 133, 141
Mundy, Harry 56

Needell, Tiff 126, 128
Nettles, John 18

Panther Rio 130, 131, 132

Raven, Clive and Gillian 6, 105, 138
Ricardo 7, 46
Rose, Howard 6, 104, 139,
Rouse, Andy 124
Rover 6, 8, 16, 17, 30, 31, 51, 64, 111, 113, 115, 123
Rover 200 and Vitesse 31, 115

Saab 14, 44, 46–48
Shepard, James 6, 116–118
Soubry, Michael 6, 50–55
ST (Special Tuning) 119, 121
Standard Motor Company 7, 8, 16–22, 42, 43, 44, 63, 86
   141

Standard models:
   Eight 8, 20, 42, 44
   Pennant 42
   Vanguard 8, 21
Snetterton Circuit 126
Stockley, Terry and Guy 6, 81, 82–84
Syer, Johnson 122

TAP Rally 122
Thruxton Circuit 126
Triumph models:
   1800/2000 7, 18
   2000 8, 9, 11, 16, 17, 21, 22, 24, 30, 32, 33, 40, 54, 67,
    72, 74, 78, 79, 81, 86, 95, 119, 121
   Acclaim 8, 16, 30, 31, 114, 115
   GT6 63
   Herald 8, 9, 11, 18, 20, 21, 22, 24, 43, 44, 60, 63, 74, 87,
    89 138, 139
   Mayflower 7, 19, 42
   Pony 63, 64, 119
   Renown 18, 19
   Roadster 7, 18, 19
   Spitfire 9, 16, 22, 24, 43, 44, 111, 119
   TR2-3 7, 19, 20
   TR4/4a 9, 19, 20, 22
   TR5 110
   TR6 101, 131
   TR10 46
   Vitesse 16, 21, 63

Unipart 6, 125–128

Vandervell 126, 128
Vauxhall 14, 16, 24, 45, 124

Wood, Paul 6, 108–109
Webster, Harry 24, 35, 45, 61, 78, 141

Ypres Rally 122